Italia
Cours

Elisabeth S

For UK order enquiries: please contact Bookpoint Ltd,
130 Milton Park, Abingdon, Oxon OX14 4SB.
Telephone: +44 (0) 1235 827720. *Fax:* +44 (0) 1235 400454.
Lines are open 09.00–17.00, Monday to Saturday, with a 24-hour
message answering service. Details about our titles and how to
order are available at www.teachyourself.com

For USA order enquiries: please contact McGraw-Hill
Customer Services, PO Box 545, Blacklick, OH 43004-0545, USA.
Telephone: 1-800-722-4726. *Fax:* 1-614-755-5645.

For Canada order enquiries: please contact McGraw-Hill
Ryerson Ltd, 300 Water St, Whitby, Ontario L1N 9B6, Canada.
Telephone: 905 430 5000. *Fax:* 905 430 5020.

Long renowned as the authoritative source for self-guided
learning – with more than 50 million copies sold worldwide –
the Teach Yourself series includes over 500 titles in the fields
of languages, crafts, hobbies, business, computing and education.

British Library Cataloguing in Publication Data: a catalogue
record for this title is available from the British Library.

Library of Congress Catalog Card Number: on file.

First published in UK 2004 by Hodder Education, part of Hachette
UK, 338 Euston Road, London NW1 3BH.

First published in US 2004 by The McGraw-Hill Companies, Inc.

This edition published 2010.

The *Teach Yourself* name is a registered trade mark of
Hodder Headline.

Typeset by MPS Limited, A Macmillan Company.

Printed in Great Britain for Hodder Education, an Hachette UK
Company, 338 Euston Road, London NW1 3BH, by CPI Cox &
Wyman, Reading, Berkshire RG1 8EX.

The publisher has used its best endeavours to ensure that the URLs
for external websites referred to in this book are correct and active
at the time of going to press. However, the publisher and the author
have no responsibility for the websites and can make no guarantee
that a site will remain live or that the content will remain relevant,
decent or appropriate.

Hachette UK's policy is to use papers that are natural, renewable
and recyclable products and made from wood grown in sustainable
forests. The logging and manufacturing processes are expected to
conform to the environmental regulations of the country of origin.

Impression number   10 9 8 7 6 5 4 3 2 1

Year   2014 2013 2012 2011 2010

Contents

Read this first

Read this first – and meet your personal tutor!

Teaching yourself a foreign language can be quite difficult, because:

- ▶ There's no one to talk to
- ▶ There's no one to correct you
- ▶ There's no one to tell you if you are doing well

That's why the **Italian starter kit** comes with a built-in **personal tutor**. So you are never left on your own or tempted to give up.

With your **tutor** at your side you'll work through your daily programme of listening, learning, speaking, and more speaking, until you get it right. But it's all quick and easy.

There are hardly any written exercises in this book. After all, you want to *speak* Italian, not hand over pieces of paper, to find out where the shops are.

At the end of each week your **tutor** will check your speaking progress. You'll be amazed at the result!

On Day 1 you'll meet Paul and Claire. They are fed up with the bad weather and are off to Italy. They do the things most people do – shopping, eating out, sightseeing, even looking at property and going to the doctor's. As they speak Italian to each other all the time (aren't they clever!), you'll pick up all the important words which *you* will want to use. That's how easy it is.

There's only one thing you must do: follow the daily programme as suggested. Go straight to **What to do today** and work your way down. Don't skip bits. Everything is there for a purpose: to get you to speak fluently – fast!

Now read the next page, and then you are ready to begin.

Start with the first **CD** and meet your **tutor!**

CD1	CD2
Introduction: Track 1	Week 3 (from Day 7):
Week 1: Tracks 2–8	Track 1
Week 2: Tracks 9–15	Week 4: Tracks 2–8
Week 3 (to Day 6):	Week 5: Tracks 9–15
Tracks 16–21	Week 6: Tracks 16–22
	Week 7: Tracks 23–29

Recorded at Alchemy Mastering, London W1. Cast: Luca Bottale, Gianmarco Ceconi, Daniela Fava, Andy Johnson, Lara Parmiani. Musical interludes kindly provided by Francisco Lucas.

Why this Starter kit works

🔊 **CD1, TR 1**

With this Starter kit anyone can learn Italian in just seven weeks. Because …

- ✓ There are only **210 Italian words** in the whole coursebook. That's enough for basic communication.
- ✓ You learn **five new words a day**. That's manageable. Anyone can learn **five** words in a day!
- ✓ You have **Flash cards** to help you. They make learning less boring as you 'turn and learn' and reshuffle the pack.
- ✓ You start **speaking in whole sentences** from Day 1. That's what you want.
- ✓ There's no complicated grammar, just a few **Nuts and bolts**. They'll help you put things together.
- ✓ You'll learn to say things by heart. That's most important. It will make you **speak fluently – fast**. So talk to the dog, to the fridge or to the unsuspecting offspring – OUT LOUD! This will speed up the sentence's journey from your brain to your mouth.

And best of all …

- ✓ There's your **personal tutor** on the two **CD**s, guiding, explaining, motivating and testing, and making sure you'll do well on the **Progress chart**.

There's also some 'first aid' in the **Kit**, a booklet with lots of additional and useful information on **shopping**, **eating out** and **travelling**, even some **medical advice** plus a **mini-dictionary** of all your new words. This is your **Traveller's companion** for you to keep in your bag or your pocket when you are off to Italy.

Finally, when you have finished the course, filled in your **Certificate** and are back from your trip I'd love to hear from you. You can write to me c/o Hodder Education, or e-mail me at esmith@mercuryin.es.

Good luck, and … Arrivederci!

Elizabeth Smith

The author would like to thank Paola Tite, who acted as language consultant in the preparation of this book.

Progress chart

This is where you record your weekly result and watch your progress.

Each week write your score in one of the boxes. If your score is less than 60% – highly unlikely! – spend an extra day going over the New words and the exercises of that week. Then take the Day 7 test again.

	60–70%	71–80%	81–90%	91–100%
Week 1	✓			
Week 2				
Week 3				
Week 4				
Week 5				
Week 6				
Week 7				

At the end of the course throw out your worst score. (We all have a bad week at times.) Then add up the remaining six scores. Divide the total by 6 to get your average score.

Total of six scores _____ **divided by 6**
= my final score (⎵) **%**

Match up your final score with one of these:

60–70% = good   71–80% = very good
81–90% = excellent   91%+ = outstanding

You are now ready to write your course result on your **Certificate** at the back of the book.

Congratulations!

Only got a minute?

If you only have one minute spare, have a look at the following.

Would you like to meet and greet someone?

To say *hello* in Italian use **ciao**.

Good morning or *good day* is **buongiorno**.

Going home and want to say *goodbye*?

Say **arrivederci** or **ciao** again if it's an informal *cheers* and if you are meeting again soon.

And if you get stuck you could always ask **Parla inglese?** *Do you speak English?*

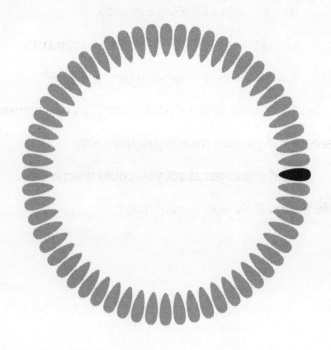

Week 1

Andiamo in Italia
Let's go to Italy

The story ...
* *A Sunday evening in February. It is cold and dark. It is raining. Paul and Claire are fed up. Then Paul has a brillliant idea ...!*

Day 1

◆ CD1, TR 2

WHAT TO DO TODAY

- ✓ Listen to **Welcome to the Italian starter kit** on the first **CD**
- ✓ Listen to today's **Story** and the **New words**
- ✓ Listen to **How to say Italian words**
- ✓ Learn today's five **New words** in the box, the ones on the left-hand side, using the **Flash cards** in the **Kit**
- ✓ Learn the **Story** by heart and say it OUT LOUD

The story

Paul	Andiamo in Italia!
Claire	Fantastico! Mi piace l'Italia. Il sole, il mare, il vino …
Paul	Andiamo a Venezia in aprile.

Today's new words		Tomorrow's new words	
andiamo	*let's go, we go*	aprile	*April*
in	*to, in*	mi piace	*I like*
l'Italia	*Italy*	il sole	*the sun*
fantastico	*fantastic, great*	il mare	*the sea, seaside*
a	*to, in*	il vino	*the wine*

piace – c + e or i = " ch" sound

2

Day 2

WHAT TO DO TODAY

- ✓ **Nuts and bolts:** Listen to the **CD**, then read and – learn them
- ✓ Listen to the **CD – Story** and **New words**
- ✓ Listen to the **New sentences**
- ✓ Listen to **How to say Italian words**
- ✓ Learn today's five **New words** in the box, the ones on the right-hand side, using the **Flash cards**
- ✓ Learn the **New sentences** by heart and say them OUT LOUD

Yesterday's new words		Today's new words	
andiamo	*let's go, we go*	aprile	*April*
in	*to, in*	mi piace	*I like*
l'Italia	*Italy*	il sole	*the sun*
fantastico	*fantastic, great*	il mare	*the sea, seaside*
a	*to, in*	il vino	*the wine*

Today's new sentences
Andiamo in Italia, a Venezia. Andiamo in aprile. Mi piace il sole, mi piace il mare. Il vino in Italia? Fantastico!

NUTS AND BOLTS

In Italia, a Venezia. Mi piace l'Italia.

When you go *to a country* you say **in: in Italia** *to Italy*.

When you go *to a place* in a country you say **a: a Venezia** *to Venice*.

When you speak about Italy, you always say *the Italy* **l'Italia**.

I like Italy.   **Mi piace l'Italia.**

Day 3

WHAT TO DO TODAY

✓ Listen to the **Story** and the **New words**. Listen again until you can say all the words correctly
✓ Learn the **New words** in the box. Use the **Flash cards**
✓ Listen to the **New sentences**
✓ **Nuts and bolts**: Listen to the **CD**, then read and ... learn them
✓ Learn the **New sentences** by heart and say them OUT LOUD
✓ **Let's speak Italian!** Do the exercise on the next page and say the sentences OUT LOUD. Then check them on the **CD**

The story
Claire   Ma non abbiamo molti soldi ...

Today's new words	
ma	*but*
non	*don't, not*
abbiamo	*we have*
molto, molti	*much, many*
soldi, molti soldi	*money, a lot of money*

Today's new sentences
Mi piace il vino. Ma – abbiamo soldi? Soldi? Non molti.

NUTS AND BOLTS

Negatives and questions
To turn something positive into something negative just add **non**.
Put **non** in front of the verb.

We have money.	**Abbiamo soldi.**
We don't have money. =	**Non abbiamo soldi.**
Not we have money.	

To turn a statement into a question just use your voice to make it sound like a question.

We are going to Venice.   **Andiamo a Venezia.**
Are we going to Venice?   **Andiamo a Venezia?**

LET'S SPEAK ITALIAN!

Say these sentences OUT LOUD and then turn each into the negative, like this:

Mi piace il sole. → Non mi piace il sole.

Now over to you:

- Andiamo in aprile.
- Mi piace il mare.
- Abbiamo molto vino.
- Andiamo a Roma.
- Abbiamo soldi.
- Andiamo a Rimini?

Day 4

🔊 **CD1, TR 5**

WHAT TO DO TODAY

- ✓ Listen to the **Story** and the **New words**. Listen again until you can say all the words correctly
- ✓ Listen to the **New sentences**
- ✓ Listen to **How to say Italian words**
- ✓ **Nuts and bolts:** Listen to the **CD**, then read and … learn them
- ✓ Learn the five **New words** in the box. Use the **Flash cards** to make it easy
- ✓ Learn the **New sentences** by heart and say them OUT LOUD
- ✓ **Let's speak Italian!** Say the sentences OUT LOUD and then check them on the **CD**

The story
Paul   Ah, ho un amico, Carlo Rossi. Ha una casa a Venezia.
Claire   Una casa a Venezia? Fantastico!

Today's new words

ho	*I have*
un, una	*a*
un amico, un'amica	*a male friend, a female friend*
ha	*he/she/it has, you have*
una casa, la casa	*a house, the house*

h is silent

Today's new sentences
Ho una casa al mare. Carlo ha un'amica ma non mi piace molto.

NUTS AND BOLTS

avere *have, to have*
I, you, he, she, it, we or *they* are not much used in Italian. You tell WHO is doing something by the verb and very often by the end of the verb. **Ho** means *I have*. **Abbiamo** means *we have*. So the **o** at the

Ha molti vino nel Casa . fantastico
rotta

6

end means *I ...(have)* and the **iamo** at the end means *we ...(have)*.
Ha can mean *he/she/it has* or *you have*.

Carlo Rossi (he) has a Ferrari.   **Carlo Rossi ha una Ferrari.**

If I met Carlo Rossi I might say to him:

Wow! You have a Ferrari,   **Wow! Ha una Ferrari, Signor**
Mr Rossi.   **Rossi.**

Finally, if you want to say *they have*, it's **hanno.**

Now have a quick look at the **Traveller's companion**. In the verbs
section you'll find the most important verbs, all neatly lined up
with their four variations.

Turn two into one
Italians love their language to be smooth. Little pairs like *to-the,*
at-the or *in-the* sound too 'staccato' to them so they prefer to 'melt'
the two words into one. Here are some combinations to give you a
feel for them.

a + il = **al**, a + la = **alla**, a + l' = **all'**, in + il = **nel**,
in + la = **nella**, in+ l' = **nell'**

Try them out in the next exercise!

LET'S SPEAK ITALIAN!

Say these sentences in Italian OUT LOUD.

▶ I have a friend, Carlo.
▶ We have a house by (at) the sea.
▶ Do we have a house by (at) the sea?
▶ Giovanni (he) has a lot of money.
▶ They don't have a house in Siena.
▶ I don't have a girlfriend in Italy.
▶ You have money, but not much.
▶ She has a lot of wine in the house. Great!

[handwritten notes:]
Ho un amico, Carlo
Abbiamo una casa
al mare,
Giovanni ha multi
soldi
non hanno una casa
a Siena
non ha una
amica in Italia
Ha soldi, ma non molti

Day 5

CD1, TR 6

WHAT TO DO TODAY

- ✓ Listen to the **Story** and the **New words**
- ✓ Listen to the **New sentences**
- ✓ Learn the **New words** with the **Flash cards**
- ✓ **Nuts and bolts**: Listen to the CD, then read and ... learn them
- ✓ Learn the **New sentences** by heart and say them OUT LOUD
- ✓ **Let's speak Italian!** Complete the sentences. Say them OUT LOUD. Then check them on the **CD**

The story

Claire Ma come andiamo? In aereo? È caro in aprile.

Paul Sì, l'aereo è caro. Non ho un amico all'Alitalia.

Today's new words

come	*how*
l'aereo	*the aeroplane*
è	*he/she/it is, you are*
caro	*expensive*
sì	*yes*

Today's new sentences

Il vino in aereo non mi piace. Com'è? È caro. Sì, è molto caro.

NUTS AND BOLTS

Mi piace

Mi piace means *I like*, or *I like it, him, her.*

> *I like the sea.* **Mi piace il mare.**

Non mi piace means *I don't like, I don't like it, him, her.*

If you don't like something or someone you'll either put the person or the thing in front of **non mi piace** or after it.

I don't like Lara. **Lara non mi piace.**
I don't like (the) wine. **Non mi piace il vino.**

More contracting
Did you notice? **Una amica** became **un'amica. Come è?** *How is?* became **com'è?** And **alla Alitalia** changed to **all'Alitalia.** Much smoother.

LET'S SPEAK ITALIAN!

1 Put the right word in the gap and say the sentences OUT LOUD.

▶ Il vino non _mc_ piace.
▶ Come _____ in Italia? *andiamo*
▶ L'aereo è _____. *caso*
▶ Giovanni _ha_ una casa al mare.

2 Now tell me in Italian that you like

▶ Italy *mi piace l'Italia*
▶ Portofino *mi piace Portofino*
▶ the sea *mi piace il mare*
▶ the wine *mi piace il vino*

and that you do not like

▶ Rimini *Rimini non mi piace*
▶ the sun *Non mi piace il sole*
▶ the aeroplane *Non mi piace l'aereo*
▶ the house *Non mi piace la casa*

Day 6

WHAT TO DO TODAY

✓ Listen to the **Story** and the **New words**
✓ Learn the **New words**, using the **Flash cards**. You now know your first 30 Italian words (and a few extras)!
✓ Learn the **New sentences** by heart and say them OUT LOUD
✓ Listen to **How to say Italian words**
✓ **Nuts and bolts**: Listen to the **CD**, then read and … learn them
✓ **Let's speak Italian!** Say the sentences below OUT LOUD and then check them on the **CD**

The story

Claire Abbiamo la macchina. Andiamo in macchina. Non è molto caro. No. È economico.

Paul Sì, andiamo in macchina. È molto economico. Ma … la macchina è rotta!

Today's new words

la macchina	*the car*
molto	*very*
no	*no*
economico	*cheap*
rotto, rotta	*broken, out of order*

Today's new sentences

Un'amica a Venezia ha una macchina. Mi piace molto. Ma è molto cara. Abbiamo una macchina economica. Com'è la macchina? Rotta? Sì, è rotta.

NUTS AND BOLTS

Names of things – nouns

There are two kinds of nouns in Italian: masculine and feminine. You can tell which is which by the word **il** or **la,** or **un** or **una**, in front of the word. Most of the time you can also tell by the ending of the noun.

Most masculine nouns end in **-o**:

il vino, un amico

Most feminine nouns end in **-a**:

la casa, una macchina

And if there is a word to describe the noun (the adjective), like **fantastico** or **rotto** it follows behind, taking the same ending. So it sort of rhymes along:

il vino fantastico	*a great wine*
una **cas**a **car**a	*an expensive house*

When you talk about more than one thing (plural) the **il** and **la** change into **i** and **le**. And to complete the jigsaw, all words ending in **o** and **a** now end in **i** and **e**:

i vini fantastici	*the great wines*
le **cas**e **car**e	*the expensive houses*

Some nouns end in **e**, so you can't tell what they are. Look at the **il** or **la** in front of them. Then you'll know. The plural of **e** is **i**:

il mare, i mari	*the sea, the seas*

This may sound complicated but it is really easy, and you'll learn it without even noticing. Best of all, if occasionally you get muddled and say 'il casa caro' or 'le vini fantastico', the Italians won't throw a fit but will understand you perfectly!

Tip of the day

> **in macchina** *by car*   **in aereo** *by plane*

LET'S SPEAK ITALIAN!

Say in Italian:

- The wine is not cheap.
- It is very expensive.
- We have a broken car.
- How is the house?
- You have many friends.
- Let's go by car, not by plane.
- I like Angelo. But he is in Italy.
- Does Marco have a girlfriend? (**amica**)
- Do you have a cheap car?
- We have an expensive house at the sea.

il vino non e economico

E molto caro

Abbiamo una macchina rotta

Com è La casa?

Ha multi amici

Abbiamo in macchina, non in aereo

Mi pace Angela. Ma è a l'Itala

Marco ha un'amica?

Ha una macchina economica?

Abbiamo una casa cara al sole mare

Day 7

WHAT TO DO TODAY

Today you are going to do a lot of talking. First, listen to the whole **Story**, then read it OUT LOUD. Then do the two practice rounds below, and finally test yourself. You'll be surprised at how much Italian you know already, after just ONE week!

> **Here's this week's whole story ...**
>
> **Paul**   Andiamo in Italia!
>
> **Claire**   Fantastico! Mi piace l'Italia. Il sole, il mare, il vino ...
>
> **Paul**   Andiamo a Venezia in aprile.
>
> **Claire**   Ma non abbiamo molti soldi ...
>
> **Paul**   Ah, ho un amico, Carlo Rossi. Ha una casa a Venezia.
>
> **Claire**   Una casa a Venezia? Fantastico! Ma come andiamo? In aereo? È caro in aprile.
>
> **Paul**   Sì, l'aereo è caro. Non ho un amico all'Alitalia.
>
> **Claire**   Abbiamo la macchina. Andiamo in macchina. Non è molto caro. No. È economico.
>
> **Paul**   Sì, andiamo in macchina. È molto economico. Ma ... la macchina è rotta!

TELL ME, TELL ME (IN ITALIAN!) THAT ...

▶ you (and your friend) are going to Italy. (**Andiamo ...**)

▶ you are going by car, you are not going in the plane, the plane is out of order.

▶ you have a friend, Maria, in Pescara. Maria has a house.

▶ you are going to the sea, in the sun, the wine is very cheap.

▶ you like Italy very much!

When you have said it all OUT LOUD, listen to the **CD** and check it.

TELL ME MORE …

Answer these questions, starting with **sì** *yes* and then again with **no**, like this:

> La casa è economica?
> Sì, la casa è economica. No, la casa non è economica.

Remember: The Italians say: The house *not is* cheap. The *not* goes before the verb **è**.

Now you try:

- ▶ La casa è al mare?
- ▶ Com'è la casa, cara?
- ▶ Andiamo in macchina in aprile?
- ▶ Ho molti amici in Italia?
- ▶ La macchina è rotta?

Now listen to the **CD** and check if your answers were right. If you got into a muddle just do it again.

IN A FLASH

Now take out the five **Flash sentences** and with the English facing you, say the Italian – in a flash! Then turn the card over and check.

TESTING, TESTING

Close the book and listen one more time to the whole **Story** of Day 7. Then, without looking at the Flash cards, write down all the Italian words you can remember. Score 50% for remembering 15 words and then 5% for each additional word. If you remember 25 words or more you'll score 100%.

YOUR RESULT THIS WEEK

Write your score for the week here:

My score ___70___ **%**   **Date** _____

Now mark up your **Progress chart**.

FINALLY ...

Italian people will really appreciate your making an effort to speak their language and are full of praise when you try. They don't mind at all if you make mistakes.

Week 2

Dov'è Gina?
Where's Gina?

The story continues ...

* *On arrival at Venice airport Paul and Claire fight their way through the crowds. They are looking for Gina, Carlo's girlfriend, whom they have not met before.*

Day 1

CD1, TR 9

WHAT TO DO TODAY

- ✓ Read today's five **New words**
- ✓ Read and work out the **Story** and the **New sentences**
- ✓ Listen to the **New words**, the **Story** and the **New sentences** on the **CD**
- ✓ **Nuts and bolts:** Listen to the **CD**, then read and ... learn them
- ✓ Learn today's five **New words** and the five **New sentences** by heart
- ✓ Say the **New sentences** OUT LOUD
- ✓ Test yourself with **Let's speak Italian!**, then check your answers with the **CD**

The story
(In the arrival hall at Venice airport)

Claire   Dov'è Gina? Non è qui.
Paul   No, non è qui. C'è molta gente qui. Non mi piace.
             Andiamo all'autobus.

Today's new words

dove	*where*
qui	*here*
c'è, ci sono	*there is, there are*
la gente	*the people*
l'autobus	*the bus*

Today's new sentences
Dov'è il mare? È qui? No, non è qui. C'è un autobus qui? Sì, ma c'è molta gente nell'autobus.

18

NUTS AND BOLTS

C'è *there is/is there?* **Ci sono** *there are/are there?*
You'll hear these words a lot. They are very useful when you are looking for something like a bus, a taxi, a bank or a shop.

Is there a bus here? **C'è un autobus qui?**
Where are there taxis? **Dove ci sono taxi?**

Nell'autobus *in the bus*
Just a reminder: **in + l'** contracts to **nell'**. Hell's bells!

Al mare *to the seaside*
Another contraction: **a + il** becomes **al**. And **a + la** becomes one word: **alla**.

LET'S SPEAK ITALIAN!

1 Say these sentences in Italian OUT LOUD and practise using **c'è** and **ci sono**:

▶ Is there wine? *c'è vino?*
▶ No, there is no wine. *no, non c'è vino*
▶ Are there people here? *c'è sono gente qui?*
▶ Yes, there are people here. *sì, ci sono gente qui*

2 Now practise **al, all', alla, nel, nell'** and **nella** and say in Italian:

▶ Let's go to the bus. *Andiamo all'autobus*
▶ Let's go to the seaside. *Andiamo al mare*
▶ Gina is in the bus. *Gina è nell'autobus*
▶ Are we going to the car? *Andiamo alla macchina?*
▶ Is Luigi in the car? (Say: Luigi is in the car?) *Luigi è nella macchina?*
▶ Carlo is in the taxi. *carlo è nell taxi*

Day 2

CD1, TR 10

WHAT TO DO TODAY

- ✓ Read today's five **New words**
- ✓ Read and work out the **Story** and the **New sentences** and listen to it all on the **CD**
- ✓ Learn today's five **New words** and the **New sentences** by heart
- ✓ Speak to me! Do the three lots of **Let's speak Italian!**
- ✓ Check your progress with the **CD**

The story

Claire   Un momento, forse Gina è qui, a destra. No, non è qui. Andiamo in taxi?

Paul   No! Non andiamo in taxi. È molto caro. Andiamo in autobus.
(*To a stranger*) Scusi, dove c'è un autobus per Venezia?

Today's new words

un momento	*a moment*
forse	*perhaps*
a destra	*on the right*
scusi	*excuse me*
per	*for*

Today's new sentences

L'autobus per Venezia è molto economico. Ah sì? Scusi, dov'è?
Qui a destra.

LET'S SPEAK ITALIAN!

Say in Italian:

▶ Where is the wine? I like it. Is it perhaps in the car?
▶ Where is the car? The car is in Italy.
▶ Is there a bus for Pisa? No, there isn't a bus for Pisa.
  There is a bus for Lucca.
▶ Is it expensive? No, it is cheap.
▶ Where are the people? Excuse me, a moment, the people?
  Perhaps they are in the bus.

AND SPEAK SOME MORE ITALIAN ...

Now make up four questions starting with **Scusi, dov'è ...?** and
Scusi, dove sono ...? Then alternate your answers with **qui** and
a destra. For example:

Scusi, dov'è l'aereo? L'aereo è qui.
Scusi, dove sono i taxi? I taxi sono a destra.

▶ la macchina
▶ i soldi
▶ il sole
▶ la gente

No marks for saying it in your head or whispering. Speak
OUT LOUD!

AND SPEAK EVEN MORE ITALIAN!

Last week you learned the four forms of *have*: *I have* **ho**, *you have* **ha**, *he/she/it has* **ha** (again) and *they have* **hanno**.

Ask in Italian and then answer in Italian with both 'yes' and 'no'. For example:

Do you have a friend?	**Ha un amico?**
	Sì, ho un amico.
	No, non ho un amico.

Now ask and answer in Italian. Don't forget to speak OUT LOUD.

- ▶ Does she have a car?
- ▶ Do you have a house?
- ▶ Do they have a bus?
- ▶ Does he have money?

Day 3

WHAT TO DO TODAY

- ✓ Read today's five **New words**
- ✓ Read and work out today's **Story** with the **New sentences**. Listen to it all on the **CD**
- ✓ **Nuts and bolts**: Listen to the **CD**, then read and … learn them
- ✓ Learn today's five **New words**. Then listen to the **New sentences** and learn them by heart
- ✓ **Let's speak Italian!** It's your speaking practice – so speak OUT LOUD!
- ✓ Check your progress with the **CD**

The story

Gina   C'è un autobus qui, a sinistra. Ma … Lei, non è Paul? … Sono Gina, Gina Pavarotti!

Paul   Gina! Sì, sono Paul. Come sta? Ecco Claire!

Today's new words

a sinistra	*on the left*
Lei	*you*
sono	*I am*
come sta?	*how are you?*
ecco	*here is, here are*

Today's new sentences

Sono (*give your name*). Lei è Carlo Rossi? Come sta? Lei ha una macchina? Dov'è? A sinistra. Andiamo! Ecco la macchina. Fantastico!

NUTS AND BOLTS

Lei *you*

This is a polite and formal way of saying *you* when you speak to one person. Normally you don't need to use **Lei**.

> *You have a car.*   **Ha una macchina.**

You only use it when you want to stress the *you* or want to make sure there is no confusion between *you* and *he/she/it*.

> *Oh, it's <u>you</u>!*   **È Lei!**
> *<u>You</u> have a car!*   **Lei ha una macchina!**

as opposed to <u>he</u> or <u>she</u> *has a car* which is also **ha una macchina**.

The informal way of saying *you* is **tu**, when you speak to one person, or **voi**, when you speak to more than one person. They are mostly used for family and friends and need a lot of extra grammar! We'll avoid them in this **Starter kit!**

Qui *here*, **ecco** *here is, here are*
Qui is the normal word for *here*.

> *The car is here.*   **La macchina è qui.**

But if you wanted to say *Here's the car!*, you would use **ecco**.

> *Here is the car!*   **Ecco la macchina!**

You often use **ecco** when there's an element of surprise or when you are presenting something.

> *Here's Claire!*   **Ecco Claire!**

LET'S SPEAK ITALIAN!

1 Say in Italian:

▶ The bus is broken.
▶ Maria is a friend.
▶ I am Jenny/Richard. I am in the aeroplane.
▶ The house is on the left.
▶ Are *you* Giovanni? Are *you* in Pescara?
▶ Where is Paolo? He isn't here.
▶ Here's the bus!

2 Put the right word in the gap and say the sentence OUT LOUD. Choose from:

dov', per, forse, sono, ha, qui, scusi, sinistra

▶ La gente qui _____ molti soldi.
▶ _____ è il mare? A destra? No, a _____.
▶ _____ Paola Versaci. Come sta?
▶ Andiamo a Verona?Ah, _____ in aprile.
▶ _____, dov'è l'autobus _____ Roma?
▶ Non sono in Inghilterra (*England*), sono _____, in Italia!

Day 4

CD1, TR 12

WHAT TO DO TODAY

✓ Read today's five **New words**
✓ Read and work out the **Story** and the **New sentences**
✓ Listen to it all on the **CD**
✓ Look at the **Traveller's companion**. In the **What you need to know** section you'll find the **names of the months**. Listen to the **CD**, and read along OUT LOUD
✓ Learn today's five **New words**. Then learn the **New sentences** by heart
✓ Speaking practice – always OUT LOUD: say the **New sentences** and then do the exercise in **Let's speak Italian!**
✓ Listen to the **Speaking practice** on the **CD**

The story

Claire	Buongiorno, Gina! Come sta?
Gina	Molto bene, grazie. Mi dispiace, non ho la macchina. È rotta. Ma c'è un autobus … fra due ore.

Today's new words

buongiorno	*good morning, good day*
molto bene	*very well*
grazie, molte grazie	*thank you, thank you very much*
mi dispiace	*I am sorry*
due ore, fra due ore	*two hours, in two hours*

Today's new sentences
Buongiorno! Come sta? Molto bene, grazie. Ma Angelo non sta bene. Ah, mi dispiace!

LET'S SPEAK ITALIAN!

Here are 12 great destinations: Roma, Siena, Firenze, Genova, Sicilia, Sardegna, Milano, Amalfi, San Remo, Cortina d'Ampezzo, Bologna, Lago Maggiore. When you know the months join month and destination with **andiamo** like this:

In gennaio andiamo a Roma.

Day 5

WHAT TO DO TODAY

✓ Read today's five **New words**
✓ Read and work out the **Story** and the **New sentences**. Listen to it all on the **CD**
✓ Listen to **How to say Italian words**
✓ Look at the **Traveller's companion**: Learn the essential verb **volere** (*to want*)
✓ Learn today's five **New words** and the **New sentences** by heart
✓ Say the **New sentences** OUT LOUD
✓ **Nuts and bolts**: Listen to the **CD**, then read and ... learn them
✓ **Let's speak Italian!** Do the exercise and practise **volere**
✓ Check your speaking practice with the **CD**

The story

Claire	Fra due ore! Andiamo al bar. Voglio un brandy.
Paul	Un brandy? No! ... (*to the barman*) Prego, due cappuccini. E per Lei, Gina?
Gina	Un cappuccino e ... forse ... un whisky, per favore.

Today's new words

un bar	*a bar, a café*
voglio	*I want*
prego	*please, you are welcome*
e	*and*
per favore	*please*

Today's new sentences

Prego, voglio un cappuccino e una Coca Cola. E dov'è l'autobus, per favore? Andiamo a Torino fra due ore.

28

NUTS AND BOLTS

Prego or **per favore?**
Both mean *please* – so what's the difference? You'll hear **prego** a lot when people ask for things like coffee or snacks or items in a shop. **Prego, un cappuccino ...** When things have been handed over you'll hear **grazie** *thank you* and then **prego** again by the waiter or shop assistant, now meaning *You are welcome!*

Per favore is more general and a little stronger.

Finally, don't be surprised if the waiter or shop assistant greets you with **Prego, signore/signora?** meaning *Can I help you?*

LET'S SPEAK ITALIAN!

Say in Italian:

- ▶ I want a cappuccino.
- ▶ You want an expensive car.
- ▶ He wants a cheap house.
- ▶ She wants a fantastic friend.
- ▶ We want a lot of money.
- ▶ They want a taxi.
- ▶ Do you want the bus for Milan?
- ▶ We want a house, but at the seaside.
- ▶ We don't want the sun.
- ▶ Antonio does not want a lot of people in the house.

Now say it again – fast!

Voglio
vuole
Vogliamo
Vogliono

Day 6

WHAT TO DO TODAY

✓ Learn the **numbers from 1 to 10** in the **Traveller's companion**
✓ Read today's five **New words**
✓ Read and work out the **Story** and the **New sentences**
✓ Listen to it all on the **CD**
✓ Listen to **How to say Italian words.** Last practice round!
✓ Learn today's **New words** and the **New sentences** by heart
✓ Take a quick look at **Nuts and bolts.** One minute will do
✓ **Let's speak Italian!** Now *you* do the talking
✓ Check your progress with the **CD**

The story

Paul	Il conto, per favore. Mamma mia! È molto caro! Tre caffè e un whisky. Un conto di dieci euro!
Claire	Andiamo all'autobus. E i biglietti? Nell'autobus?
Paul	Sì, nell'autobus. *(To the driver)* Due per Venezia, per favore.
Gina	Scusi, Paul. Non ho soldi per il biglietto. Ha quattro euro, per favore?

Today's new words

il conto	*the bill*
il caffè	*the coffee*
mamma mia!	*oh dear!*
di	*of*
il biglietto	*the ticket*

Today's new sentences

I biglietti sono economici. Otto euro per due. Ma il caffè è caro.
Il conto del bar? Cinque euro. Mamma mia!

---

bisogno, ciao, Gianni, Mamma mia, spaghetti
'Mamma mia, Gianni ha bisogno di molti spaghetti! Ciao!'

HOW TO SAY ITALIAN WORDS

Listen to the **CD** and say the Italian words and the sentence in the box above.

NUTS AND BOLTS

di *of*
Here's another little word that likes to contract.

When you want to say *of the* you'll come across **del, della, dell'**
and others.

> *of the bar* **del bar,** *of the house* **della casa,**
> *of the bus* **dell'autobus**

Quite smooth, isn't it?

LET'S SPEAK ITALIAN!

1 Make up five Italian sentences. Each one must contain the two
given words. Like this:

> **non – a: Non** voglio una casa **a** Genova.

Now you:

▶ biglietto – euro
▶ conto – per
▶ l'autobus – forse

▶ la gente – dove
▶ bar – c'è

2 Numbers. Do you know your numbers up to 10? Then count up from one, using these words:

il vino, un momento, un euro, un contó, un amico, un'amica, una macchina, un biglietto, un'ora, un cappuccino

I'll start you off: **Un vino** (you say **un**, not **uno**, in front of **il** words), **due momenti, tre** ... Now do it backwards, starting with **dieci.**

Day 7

WHAT TO DO TODAY

First, here's the whole **story** for you to read once more – OUT LOUD. Then just work through the exercises that follow and collect your gold star at the end!

Here's the week's whole story ...
(In the arrival hall at Venice airport)

Claire	Dov'è Gina? Non è qui.
Paul	No, non è qui. C'è molta gente qui. Non mi piace. Andiamo all'autobus.
Claire	Un momento, forse Gina è qui, a destra. No, non è qui. Andiamo in taxi?
Paul	No! Non andiamo in taxi. È molto caro. Andiamo in autobus. *(To a stranger)* Scusi, dove c'è un autobus per Venezia?
Gina	C'è un autobus qui, a sinistra. Ma ... Lei, non è Paul? ... Sono Gina, Gina Pavarotti!
Paul	Gina! Sì, sono Paul. Come sta? Ecco Claire!
Claire	Buongiorno, Gina! Come sta?
Gina	Molto bene, grazie. Mi dispiace, non ho la macchina. È rotta. Ma c'è un autobus ... fra due ore.
Claire	Fra due ore! Andiamo al bar. Voglio un brandy.
Paul	Un brandy? No! ... *(to the barman)* Prego, due cappuccini. E per Lei, Gina?
Gina	Un cappuccino e ... forse ... un whisky, per favore.
Paul	Il conto, per favore. Mamma mia! È molto caro! Tre caffè e un whisky. Un conto di dieci euro!
Claire	Andiamo all'autobus. E i biglietti? Nell'autobus?
Paul	Sì, nell'autobus. *(To the driver)* Due per Venezia, per favore.
Gina	Scusi, Paul. Non ho soldi per il biglietto. Ha quattro euro, per favore?

Now you do the talking!

TELL ME, TELL ME (IN ITALIAN!) THAT ...

... Gina is the girlfriend of Carlo, ... she does not have the car, ... the car is out of order, ... it is with Marco in Perugia, ... there are a lot of people in the bar on the left, ... but there are not a lot of people in the bar on the right.

... Claire wants a brandy, ... Paul does not want a brandy, ... he wants a coffee, ... it is very expensive.

... the tickets for the bus are four euros, ... but Gina does not have money for the ticket.

TELL ME ABOUT YOURSELF

Tell me your name, tell me that you are from Liverpool. Tell me you like Italy. Tell me you have six friends in Sicily, they have a bar in Taormina. Tell me you have tickets for the aeroplane in May. Tell me there is a fantastic house at the seaside, but it is not very cheap. Tell me you do not like the wine, but you like the coffee in Italy. Tell me you want a car in Rome and that you want the sun for ten hours.

SAY IT IN A FLASH

Now take out the **Flash sentences** for Week 2. With the English facing you say each sentence in Italian and then check. Give yourself three points for each one that you get right. Subtract one point for each mistake. Write down your total points at the end. Did you score 15?

A MONTH TO REMEMBER

Say out loud the names of any five months you can remember. Then write them down. Check in the **Traveller's companion** and earn yourself up to ten points, two for each one that you get right. The spelling is not important as long as you can say the word correctly.

NUTS AND BOLTS STUFF

Finally, write these five lines into Italian, filling in the gaps with words you have learned so far. Then check with the book if it's correct. You can choose *and* or *but*.

- ▶ I am in _____ I have _____ and/but I want _____
- ▶ You are in _____ You have _____ and/but you want _____
- ▶ He is in _____ He has _____ and/but he wants _____
- ▶ We are in _____ We have _____ and/but we want _____
- ▶ They are in _____ They have _____ and/but they want _____

Here's an example:

Sono a <u>Milano</u>. Ho <u>molti soldi</u> e voglio <u>un taxi</u>.

Now listen to the **CD**, first to the whole **story** and then to **Tell me, tell me** and **Tell me about yourself.** How well did you do when *you* did the talking? What did you score? Give yourself ten points for *fair*, 20 points for *good* and 25 points for *very good* for each of these exercises. And don't be modest.

For **Nuts and bolts stuff** give yourself five points for every correct line. Take off one point for each mistake.

YOUR RESULT THIS WEEK

Now add up all your points:

- ✓ Tell me, tell me /25
- ✓ Tell me about yourself /25
- ✓ Say it in a flash /15
- ✓ A month to remember /10
- ✓ Nuts and bolts stuff /25

Total score /100% **Date _____**

What did you get ... 80%? 90%? 95%? ... 100%? Are you pleased with your score? Then enter it on the **Progress chart.**

Week 3

Voglio una casa ... a Venezia!
I want a house ... in Venice!

The story continues ...

- *This is the life! It's sunny and it's warm, and the beach, shops and restaurants beckon. So why not cash in those savings and get a place in the sun? Let's ask Carlo for the name of an estate agent ...*

Day 1

WHAT TO DO TODAY

✓ Read and work out the **Story**, today's five **New words** and
  the **New sentences**
✓ Listen to and speak along with the **CD**
✓ Learn today's five **New words** and the **New sentences** by heart
✓ **Nuts and bolts**: Listen to the **CD**, then read and ... learn them
✓ Look at the **Traveller's companion**. Learn the essential verbs
  andare *to go* and **comprare** *to buy*. You know most of this
  already
✓ **Let's speak Italian!** Do the three exercises to practise speaking
  OUT LOUD
✓ Check your progress on the **CD**

The story

Paul Carlo, una domanda, per favore. Ha il nome di un'agenzia
immobiliare? Voglio comprare una casa a Venezia.

Carlo Una casa a Venezia? Una casa a Venezia non è
economica, costa molto. Ci sono molte agenzie ... Sarti,
Bellini, Tozzi ... Forse Bellini ...

Today's new words

una domanda	*a question*
il nome	*the name*
un'agenzia immobiliare	*an estate agency*
comprare	*to buy*
costa	*it costs*

Today's new sentences

Scusi, Carlo, una domanda. Ha il nome di un amico con 10.000
(diecimila) euro? Voglio comprare una macchina.

NUTS AND BOLTS

Comprare *to buy*
Comprare is a so-called 'regular' verb and a very good verb to know! That means it has a standard pattern of endings – **o, a, iamo** and **ano** – telling you *who* is doing the buying. Have a look at **comprare** in the **Traveller's companion**. When you meet another regular verb, like **lavorare** *to work* or **mangiare** *to eat*, you can use the same endings. That makes life much easier!

Voglio *I want*
If you 'want something' you say **voglio** ... You learned it last week on Day 5.

> **Voglio una casa, voglio una macchina, voglio ... un whisky!**
> *I want a house, I want a car, I want ... a whisky.*

If you 'want to do something' you use **voglio** *plus* whatever you want to do. For example if you want to *buy* something you would say: **Voglio comprare ...**

> *I want to buy a car.*   **Voglio comprare una macchina.**

And when you have mastered the verb **andare** *to go* and you are bored at a party, you'll be able to say:

> *I want to go home.*   **Voglio andare a casa.**

Quite easy, really.

LET'S SPEAK ITALIAN!

1 When an Italian person speaks to you at the speed of an automatic rifle you'll probably just catch **capisce?** *do you understand?* at the end of it. Read the following sentences out loud as quickly as you can and give the meaning in English.

> Carlo va a un bar e compra un brandy. Va a Pisa in macchina. Andiamo all'agenzia immobiliare con molti soldi. Emilio e Maria vanno a casa. Comprano quattro biglietti. Non compro il vino qui. Compriamo il vino a Firenze. Non compra molto. È molto caro. Vado a Roma con un'amica.

2 Say these phrases quickly in Italian:

> I go to Italy, he buys a car, she buys the wine, it goes to the sea, we go to London (**Londra**), you buy a bus, they buy a house, he goes to the bar, we buy two cappuccinos, I buy the tickets, she goes to Bologna, they go to Sicily, you go to the agency.

3 Do you *want* something? Do you want to *do* something? Say in Italian:

▶ I want the sea. I want to go to the sea.
▶ You want the wine. You want to buy the wine.
▶ Do you want the wine? Do you want to buy the wine?
▶ Does he want a car? Does he want to buy an expensive car?
▶ We want a house. We want to buy a fantastic house.
▶ She wants Siena. She wants to go to Siena.
▶ They want the bus. They want to go in (the) bus.

Day 2

WHAT TO DO TODAY

✓ Read today's five **New words**
✓ Read and work out the **Story** and the **New sentences**
✓ Listen to and speak along with the **CD**
✓ Learn today's five **New words** and the **New sentences** by heart
✓ **Nuts and bolts:** Listen to the **CD**, then read and learn them
✓ Practise speaking with **Let's speak Italian!**
✓ Check your progress with the **CD**

The story
(Later)

Claire Buongiorno, Carlo, ... una domanda, per favore. Mi piace molto Venezia e voglio avere una casa qui. Ha il nome di un'agenzia immobiliare?

Carlo Beh ..., ci sono molte agenzie. Forse Bellini. È nel centro di Venezia. È una buona agenzia.

Today's new words

beh ...	*well ...*
avere	*to have*
il centro	*the centre*
sono	*they are*
buono	*good*

Today's new sentences
Le due agenzie immobiliari sono buone. Hanno molte case. Sono nel centro di Pisa. Beh ..., andiamo!

NUTS AND BOLTS

beh ... and ... uffa!

Beh is not really a word, it's more like a sound which the Italians make when they want a little time before speaking. It's jolly useful, especially when you want to get all your Italian words neatly lined up before you answer. You can make that sound quite long like ... **mmmmmbeh** if you need extra time. For example:

L'agenzia	Vuole comprare la casa? È cara ma fantastica!
You	Mmmmmmmmmmmmbeh. No, grazie!

Uffa! is used when you are fed up with someone or with something. 'There goes the last train without me!' **Uffa!**

LET'S SPEAK ITALIAN!

Centipedes ...

Here are some short sentences which need extra 'legs'. Make them as long as you like. Here's an example:

Short version: Voglio comprare una casa.
'Centipede' version: Voglio comprare una casa fantastica ma economica al mare, a sinistra del centro di Pisa con un'agenzia immobiliare.

Over to you! If you get stuck start again. Don't write anything down. This is *speaking* practice. You are not likely to communicate with the locals on pieces of paper!

- ▶ Voglio comprare ...
- ▶ Emilio vuole comprare un biglietto ...
- ▶ Vogliamo avere ... ma non vogliamo ...
- ▶ Non voglio andare a ...

Day 3

WHAT TO DO TODAY

✓ Read today's five **New words**
✓ Read and work out the **Story** and the **New sentences**
✓ Listen to and speak along with the **CD**
✓ Look at the **Traveller's companion** and learn the essential verbs **essere** *to be* and **vorrei** *I would like*
✓ **Nuts and bolts**: Listen to the **CD**. Then read and learn **vorrei** …
✓ Learn today's five **New words** and the **New sentences** by heart. Are you using the **Flash cards**?
✓ **Let's speak Italian!** *You* do the talking!
✓ Check your progress with the **CD**

The story

Claire *(On the phone)* Buongiorno. È l'agenzia immobiliare Bellini? Sono Claire Smith … No, non è Clairsmis. Sono Claire – Smith … No, non importa. Sono a Venezia e voglio comprare una casa. Vorrei un appuntamento con un'agenzia immobiliare … Beh, … sì… domani … Con Luigi? Grazie.

Today's new words

non importa	*it doesn't matter*
vorrei	*I would like (to)*
l'appuntamento	*the appointment*
con	*with*
domani	*tomorrow*

Today's new sentences

Sono a Milano ma vorrei andare a Como. In autobus o taxi? Non importa. Ho un appuntamento a Como con Luigi fra tre ore.

NUTS AND BOLTS

vorrei *I would like*

At times you may want to use **vorrei**, the polite *I would like*, instead of the strong **voglio** *I want*. For example:

I would like a cappuccino.	**Vorrei un cappuccino.**
I would like to buy a house.	**Vorrei comprare una casa.**
I would like to have a car.	**Vorrei avere una macchina.**

And if you are ambitious, why not copy out the other three forms of the verbs and stick them on the fridge: **vorrebbe** *you/he/she/it would like*, **vorremmo** *we would like*, **vorrebbero** *they would like*. A good way of practising that Mediterranean rrrrr.

LET'S SPEAK ITALIAN!

1 Here's an easy practice round of the verb **essere**. Say in Italian:

> We are Claire and Kate. I am Claire. Kate is a friend. She is from Bari. She wants to be in London. Paul and Tom are friends. They are in Rimini but they want to be here.

2 The words in these five sentences need shuffling about. And you need to add the odd word here and there to make sense of them.

▶ vorrei – agenzia – nome
▶ vorrebbe – centro – andare – Angela
▶ vorrebbero – appuntamento – avere – agenzia – Tom e Claire
▶ vorremmo – domani – biglietto – comprare
▶ vorrei – Portofino – essere – mare

Day 4

WHAT TO DO TODAY

✓ Read today's five **New words**
✓ Read and work out the **Story** and the **New sentences**
✓ Listen to and speak along with the **CD**
✓ **Nuts and bolts**: Listen to the **CD**, then read and learn them
✓ Learn today's five **New words** and the **New sentences** by heart
✓ Look at the **Traveller's companion**. In the **Essentials** section you'll find **Useful places and services**: something Paul and Claire might need if they're buying that holiday home …
✓ **Let's speak Italian!** Enjoy the two speaking exercises
✓ Check your progress with the **CD**

The story

Paul *(On the phone)* Pronto, Bellini? … Buongiorno. Il mio nome è Blair, Paul Blair. Sono a Venezia in vacanza con mia moglie e vorrei comprare una casa o un appartamento. Vorrei un appuntamento per domani, per favore? … Sì? … Molto bene. Molte grazie.

Today's new words

pronto	*hello (on the phone, literally: ready)*
il mio, la mia	*my*
in vacanza	*on holiday*
la moglie, mia moglie	*the wife, my wife*
un appartamento	*an apartment*

Today's new sentences

Pronto. E Lei è …? È in vacanza? Vorrebbe un appuntamento. Vuole il mio appartamento? Beh … Costa molto. Ha soldi?

NUTS AND BOLTS

il mio, la mia, i miei, le mie *my*

My goodness – four ways of saying *my*! But it looks worse than it is. Just remember that the Italians say 'the my'. So it's: *the* my friend, *the* my car, *the* my tickets and *the* my houses.

Now take *my* **mio** and rhyme along with the noun:

> il mi**o** amic**o**, la mi**a** macchin**a**, i mie**i** bigliett**i** and le mi**e** cas**e**.

Can you hear how the variations roll off the tongue quite naturally? There are exceptions: **mia moglie** *my wife* and **mio marito** *my husband*. They've obviously been used so much that they lost the **il** and **la** in the process.

LET'S SPEAK ITALIAN!

By now you have learned six **essential verbs**. Only three more and your **Verb kit** for good basic communication will be complete.

1 Here's a reminder of what you know already and a quick practice round on: **avere, essere, volere, andare, comprare**. Say these sentences in Italian and time yourself. You should be able to say them in one minute or less. If you take longer say them again.

> I don't have a ticket, we are at the seaside, they don't want the apartment, let's go on holiday!, perhaps he buys the plane, does he have two girlfriends?, it is very cheap but is it good?, I would like the sun, do they go with you?, we want to buy the wine

2 Do you remember some of the useful places which you found in the **Traveller's companion?** Pretend you are showing someone your home town. Choose from **il mio, la mia, i miei, le mie** and say in Italian:

> my bank, my schools, my church, my petrol station, my hospital, my police station, my post office, my cinema, my department store, my museums, my tourist office

Day 5

WHAT TO DO TODAY

✓ Read today's five **New words**
✓ Read and work out the **Story** and the **New sentences**
✓ Listen to and speak along with the **CD**
✓ **Nuts and bolts:** Listen to the **CD**, then read and learn them
✓ Learn today's five **New words** and the **New sentences** by heart
✓ Look at the **Traveller's companion**. There are some **shopping hints**, just in case you need to flash your credit card ...
✓ **Let's speak Italian!** ... and do the two speaking exercises
✓ Check your progress with the **CD**

The story
(The next day)

Claire Voglio fare spese. Vado in centro. Vado a comprare qualcosa. Dov'è Paul?

Carlo È con la mia macchina. C'è un problema. C'è sempre qualcosa con la macchina!

Today's new words

fare spese	*to go shopping*
vado	*I go, I'm going*
qualcosa (di)	*something*
il problema	*the problem*
sempre	*always*

Today's new sentences
Voglio fare spese. Vado con la mia amica. Voglio comprare qualcosa di fantastico per il mio amico. Ma ho sempre un problema. Non ho soldi!

NUTS AND BOLTS

Four easy footnotes

1 The Italians don't go shopping; they *make purchases* **fare spese**.

2 When they *go to do* something it's always **andare a**.

> Andiamo **a** fare spese. Mario va **a** comprare la macchina.

3 And what about **il problema**? Yes, there's an **a** at the end even though it is **il problema**. Just to tease the student.

4 When you want to say *something beautiful* or *something fantastic* you have to say **qualcosa di** in Italian. So it's **qualcosa di bello, qualcosa di fantastico**. *Something of beautiful, something of fantastic*. And the adjective must always be in the masculine ... **bello, fantastico** even though it's **qualcosa**.

LET'S SPEAK ITALIAN!

1 Read these questions out loud and then answer them in Italian.

> Vorrei andare a fare spese. E Lei?

Say that you would like to go shopping and that you always buy something in Italy.

> Vado con i miei amici a Londra. E Lei?

Say that you would like to go to London in March. Say that you would like to buy something in London for your girlfriend.

Ho un problema con la mia casa.

Say that you are sorry, but that you always have a problem with your apartment.

Vuole un appuntamento in luglio?

Say that you are always on holiday in July.

2 You are in a department store. Tell me in four sentences what clothes you and other people are buying. You can look at the **Essentials** section of the **Traveller's companion** to help you decide. Here are two examples:

Compro una maglia. La mia amica compra una gonna.

Day 6

WHAT TO DO TODAY

- ✓ Read today's five **New words**
- ✓ Read and work out the **Story** and the **New sentences**
- ✓ Listen to and speak along with the **CD**
- ✓ **Nuts and bolts**: Listen to the **CD**, then read and learn them
- ✓ Learn today's five **New words** and the **New sentences** by heart
- ✓ Speak in a flash: take out the five **Flash sentences** and, with the English side facing you, say the five sentences in Italian until you are word perfect
- ✓ Get out the **Traveller's companion**: if you are a serious shopper there is more to read in the **Essentials** section
- ✓ **Let's speak Italian!** That means *you*!
- ✓ Check your progress with the **CD**

The story
(At the estate agent's)

Luigi Buongiorno, signorina Claire, sono Luigi. Lei è in vacanza e vuole comprare una casa. Lei è di Birmingham, sì? Scusi, un momento, per favore. C'è qualcuno qui … il signor Paul. Anche lui è di Birmingham. Anche lui vuole comprare una casa.

Paul Claire! Mamma mia!

Luigi Scusi, compra una casa o due?

Today's new words

signor, signora, signorina	*Mr, Mrs, Miss*
qualcuno	*someone*
anche	*also*
lui	*he (usually used only to stress he)*
o	*or*

NUTS AND BOLTS

La signora ...

When you talk <u>about someone</u> whom you would call Mr, Mrs or
Miss, you put *the* before the title. So it's **il signor** Blair, **la signora**
Smith and **la signorina** ...Lollobrigida. But when you talk <u>to
someone</u> you drop the **il/la**:

> Scusi, signor Blair.
> Buongiorno, signora Smith.
> Grazie, signorina Lollobrigida.

Una casa fantastica – una piccola casa

In Italian adjectives usually follow the noun, but the most
frequently used ones like *big* and *small* or *good* and *bad* go *before*
the noun – just like in English!

LET'S SPEAK ITALIAN!

Ask in Italian and then make up your own answers in Italian:

- ▶ Do you want to go by car or by taxi?
- ▶ Do you want to buy one ticket or five?
- ▶ Does Mr Parella want to go on holiday or to Milan?
- ▶ Do we have an appointment with Mr Fellini or with the
  travel agent?
- ▶ Are we going to the seaside or to the centre of Pescara?
- ▶ Do you also have a problem with the chemist's and the dry
  cleaner's?

Sono Jenny, sono per
Liverpool. Mi piace l'Italia.
Ho sei amici in Sicily,
hanno un bar in Taormina.
Ho biglietti dell aero
in maggio. C'E una casa
fantastica alla mare, ma
non è economica. Mi
dispiace il vino, ma mi
piace il cafe in Italia
Voglio una macchina in
Roma, voglio il sole per
diece hora

Day 7

Today you get a break from learning: no **New words** or **New sentences**. Today it's time for you to assess your progress.

WHAT TO DO TODAY

✓ Read the week's whole **Story** out loud. You now know
  90 Italian words!
✓ Have a go at the exercises that follow

This week's whole story ...

Paul   Carlo, una domanda, per favore. Ha il nome di
           un'agenzia immobiliare? Voglio comprare una casa a
           Venezia.

Carlo Una casa a Venezia? Una casa a Venezia non è
           economica, costa molto. Ci sono molte agenzie ... Sarti,
           Bellini, Tozzi ... Forse Bellini ...

(Later)

Claire Buongiorno Carlo, ... una domanda, per favore. Mi
           piace molto Venezia e voglio avere una casa qui. Ha il
           nome di un'agenzia immobiliare?

Carlo Beh ..., ci sono molte agenzie. Forse Bellini. È nel centro
           di Venezia. È una buona agenzia.

Claire *(On the phone)* Buongiorno. È l'agenzia immobiliare
           Bellini? Sono Claire Smith ... No, non è Clairsmis. Sono
           Claire – Smith ... No, non importa. Sono a Venezia e
           voglio comprare una casa. Vorrei un appuntamento con
           un'agenzia immobiliare ... Beh, ... sì ... domani ... Con
           Luigi? Grazie.

Paul   *(On the phone)* Pronto, Bellini? ... Buongiorno. Il mio
           nome è Blair, Paul Blair. Sono a Venezia in vacanza
           con mia moglie e vorrei comprare una casa o un
           appartamento. Vorrei un appuntamento per domani,
           per favore? ... Sì? ... Molto bene. Molte grazie.

                                                        (Contd)

> *(The next day)*
> **Claire**   Voglio fare spese. Vado in centro. Vado a comprare qualcosa. Dov'è Paul?
> **Carlo**   È con la mia macchina. C'è un problema. C'è sempre qualcosa con la macchina!
> *(At the estate agent's)*
> **Luigi**   Buongiorno, signorina Claire, sono Luigi. Lei è in vacanza e vuole comprare una casa. Lei è di Birmingham, sì? Scusi, un momento, per favore. C'è qualcuno qui ... il signor Paul. Anche lui è di Birmingham. Anche lui vuole comprare una casa.
> **Paul**   Claire! Mamma mia!
> **Luigi**   Scusi, compra una casa o due?

This is the day that *you* do all the talking. Here goes:

TELL ME, TELL ME...

... that it is July and that you (yourself, Paul and Claire) are on holiday in Italy. Tell me you have the name of an estate agent and that you want to buy a house. Tell me you have an appointment for tomorrow with Luigi, at the agency.

Tell me the agency has a great house by the sea but that it is very expensive. Tell me you like a house in the centre. Tell me you want a cheap house. Tell me you do not have much money. Tell me you like the centre and there are always a lot of people in the bars.

NOW TELL ME ABOUT JULIE ...

Tell me that you have a friend, Julie. Tell me she is from Manchester, she does not have a car, she goes by bus. She wants to go to Italy in August with a friend, Mark. Tell me the friend has a lot of money and a lot of friends in Florence; they have the tickets for the plane to Pisa. Tell me Julie would like to buy two jerseys; they are good and not very expensive in Italy.

FINALLY TELL ME ABOUT THE TOZZIS ...

Tell me that there are Mr Tozzi and Mrs Tozzi, they are from Bari, they are not on holiday here, in Milan. Tell me they are always in a bar and tomorrow they want to buy the bar.

Tell me you like Mrs Tozzi, she is a good friend. Tell me you have the name of the agent for the bar. Tell me that you and Mrs Tozzi have an appointment with Umberto, at the agency, in one hour.

REMEMBER THE NUMBERS?

Try to say the numbers from 1 to 10. Only after you have said them write them down – the way you said them. Now check them against the **Traveller's companion**, and give yourself a point for every one you got right. The spelling is not important.

HOW'S YOUR MEMORY?

Take out all 90 **Flash cards** for Weeks 1 to 3. Shuffle them and pick out (without looking) any 15. Now with the English side facing you say the Italian and give yourself one point for every word you know immediately. Score 15 points for knowing them all.

Now listen to the **CD**. First to the whole **story** and then to **Tell me, tell me, Now tell me about Julie** and **Tell me about the Tozzis**. Give yourself between ten and 25 points for each of the three speaking exercises depending on how well you did.

YOUR RESULT THIS WEEK

Add up all your points:

- ✓ Tell me, tell me ...   /25
- ✓ Tell me about Julie ...   /25
- ✓ Tell me about the Tozzis ... /25
- ✓ Remember the numbers?   /10
- ✓ How's your memory?   /15

Total score   **/100%**   **Date** _____

I'll bet you scored more than 70%! Now enter your result on the
Progress chart.

Week 4

Andiamo a Firenze
Let's go to Florence

The story continues ...

- *It's time for more sightseeing – Verona or Florence? Claire opts for Florence with its famous Uffizi gallery. But later that day, after a couple of drinks, will they find a place to stay?*

Day 1

WHAT TO DO TODAY

✓ Read today's five **New words**
✓ Read and work out the **Story** and the **New sentences**
✓ Listen to and speak along with the **CD**
✓ Learn today's five **New words** and the **New sentences** by heart
✓ Look at the **Traveller's companion.** Take a look at **Getting about, not lost**
✓ **Let's speak Italian!** Over to you
✓ Check your progress with the **CD**

The story

Paul Vorrei andare a Verona o a Firenze per una notte.

Claire Andiamo a Firenze. Vorrei vedere gli Uffizi. Come andiamo? In macchina, in autobus o c'è un treno? E … quando?

Today's new words

una notte	*a night, one night*
vedere	*to see*
gli Uffizi	*the Uffizi gallery*
un treno	*a train*
quando	*when*

Today's new sentences

Vorrei vedere Roma. Com'è? Fantastica! Come andiamo? In treno. Quando andiamo? Domani, per una notte.

LET'S SPEAK ITALIAN!

1 Make up some questions, asking *Would you like to ...?* Then answer them, alternating with *Yes, I want to ...* and *No, I don't want to ...* For example:

Would you like to see the Uffizi?	**Vorrebbe vedere gli Uffizi?**
	Sì, voglio vedere gli Uffizi.
Would you like to see the sea?	**Vorrebbe vedere il mare?**
	No, non voglio vedere il mare.

Here are the questions:

▶ Would you like to go by train?
▶ Would you like to buy a ticket?
▶ Would you like to be in Tuscany (**in Toscana**)?
▶ Would you like to have a car?
▶ Would you like to see the station?
▶ Would you like to buy something?

2 What do you remember from the **Traveller's companion**? Test yourself speaking OUT LOUD. Then, if you want to, you can write down your answers and check them.

Say in Italian:

do you go? she buys, they go, we buy, the hospital, the tourist office, May, January, the chemist's, the travel agent, clothes, the department store

Day 2

WHAT TO DO TODAY

✓ Read today's **New words**
✓ Read and work out the **Story** and the **New sentences**
✓ Listen to and speak along with the **CD**
✓ Learn today's five **New words** and the **New sentences** by heart
✓ **Nuts and bolts:** Listen to the **CD**, then read and learn them
✓ **Let's speak Italian!** Speak OUT LOUD
✓ Check your progress with the **CD**

The story
Paul   Se andiamo oggi, possiamo andare in macchina.
           Perché oggi Carlo non ha bisogno della macchina.
Claire Andiamo oggi!

Today's new words

se	*if*
oggi	*today*
possiamo	*we can*
perché	*because*
ha bisogno di	*he needs*

Today's new sentences
Se andiamo al mare possiamo andare in treno o in autobus.
E perché non possiamo andare in macchina? Perché oggi Mario ha bisogno della macchina. Va a vedere una casa con la sua amica.

NUTS AND BOLTS

Ho bisogno di *I need*
To say *I need* in Italian you say, literally, *I have need of* ...

I need the car.	**Ho bisogno della macchina.**
Do you need a taxi?	**Ha bisogno di un taxi?**
We need to go home.	**Abbiamo bisogno di andare a casa.**

LET'S SPEAK ITALIAN!

1 Practise saying **perché** *because* and replace the English with the Italian.

- ▶ Non vado a Bologna *because I don't like it.*
- ▶ Non vado in macchina *because there is a very cheap bus.*
- ▶ Non compro una Lamborghini *because it is expensive.*
- ▶ Andiamo in Italia *because we have a friend in Lucca.*
- ▶ Compriamo molto vino *because we are on holiday.*

2 Here's some more practice of **bisogno di**. Say in Italian:

I need the train to Milan, you need a friend, he needs to go to Rome, we need someone here, they need the tickets.

3 Complete the missing part of the sentence and practise **se** *if*.

- ▶ *If I don't have money for a taxi* vado in autobus.
- ▶ *If we buy the house today* non costa molto.
- ▶ Se vuole andare a Londra *he needs to go by plane.*
- ▶ Se andiamo in Italia *we can buy a Fiat in Turin.*

Day 3

WHAT TO DO TODAY

✓ Read today's **New words**
✓ Read and work out the **Story** and the **New sentences**
✓ Take out the **Traveller's companion**. Have a look at **colours**.
  Try to read them out loud twice. They'll be repeated for you
  shortly on the **CD**
✓ Listen to and speak along with the **CD**
✓ Learn today's five **New words** and the **New sentences** by heart
✓ **Let's speak Italian!** Now *you* do the talking!
✓ Check your progress with the **CD**

The story
*(After visiting the Uffizi, Paul and Claire are in need of
refreshments ...)*

Paul Firenze è fantastica. Mi piace molto. Ma mi piace anche
         la birra ...

Claire Per me un bicchiere di vino bianco e ... il bagno.

Today's new words

una birra	*a beer*
per me	*for me*
un bicchiere	*a glass*
bianco	*white*
il bagno	*the bath, the toilets*

Today's new sentences
Oggi vorrei un bicchiere di vino bianco. Per me una birra, per favore.
E c'è un bagno qui?

LET'S SPEAK ITALIAN!

1 Here are some items which need a colour. Remember the colour goes after the word it describes: **una casa bianca**.

Say in Italian:

> a red wine, a blue aeroplane, a yellow car, a green bus, a brown bus, a grey ticket, a yellow sun, an orange sun, a black train, red cars, blue tickets, a grey night, a pink house, a white glass

2 Remember this week's words – all 15 so far? If you don't, go back to Day 1 of this week.

Say in Italian – rapidly:

> a night, to see, a train, when, if, today, we can, because, a beer, for me, a glass, white, the toilets, the Uffizi, he doesn't need

Now make up a short sentence with each.

Day 4

WHAT TO DO TODAY

- ✓ **Nuts and bolts:** Listen to the **CD**, then read and learn them
- ✓ Look at the **Traveller's companion.** In the **For everyday use** section you'll find some **essentials for conversation**, like *hello, excuse me, thank you, goodbye*, and many more. Have a good read through
- ✓ Read today's **New words**
- ✓ Read and work out the **Story** and the **New sentences**
- ✓ Listen to and speak along with the **CD**
- ✓ Learn today's five **New words** and the **New sentences** by heart
- ✓ **Let's speak Italian!** Do the three speaking exercises
- ✓ Check your progress with the **CD**

The story
(Several drinks later they are looking for a hotel. Let's ask someone ...)
Claire   Adesso dobbiamo cercare un albergo.
         (Turning to a stranger) Scusi, può aiutarmi, per favore?
         Cerchiamo un albergo.

Today's new words

adesso	*now*
dobbiamo	*we have to, we must*
cercare	*to look for*
un albergo	*a hotel*
può aiutarmi?	*can you help me?*

Today's new sentences
Scusi, può aiutarmi? Cerco la stazione. Dobbiamo andare a Roma adesso e non c'è un autobus.

NUTS AND BOLTS

dovere *to have to, must*
You can't do without this one! Here are examples of the four variations:

Devo andare.	*I must go.*
Deve andare adesso?	*Do you have to go now?*
Maria deve andare a Pisa.	*Maria must go to Pisa.*
Dobbiamo vedere gli Uffizi.	*We must see the Uffizi.*
Devono cercare un albergo.	*They must look for a hotel.*

LET'S SPEAK ITALIAN!

Never skip the **New sentences**. If you haven't done so today learn the three sentences by heart now. You never know when you may need one of them.

1 **Devo andare ...** Pretend you want to get out of a boring invitation. Make up some excuses starting with **Mi dispiace, ma devo andare a ... e dopo** *afterwards* ...

I must go to ... and afterwards I must buy ... and afterwards I must look for ... and afterwards I must be in ... (name of town)

2 Ask someone these questions in Italian: **Deve ...?**

Do you have to go home?
Do you have to do the shopping?
Do you have to look for the hotel?
Do you have to buy the coffee?

3 Back to the **Traveller's companion**. Pick out five favourites from the **Communication essentials** and build five sentences around them. Say these sentences OUT LOUD. Afterwards you can write them down if you want to.

Day 5

WHAT TO DO TODAY

✓ Read today's five **New words**
✓ Read and work out the **Story** and the **New sentences**
✓ Listen to and speak along with the **CD**
✓ **Nuts and bolts:** Listen to the **CD,** then read and learn them
✓ Learn today's five **New words** and the **New sentences** by heart
✓ **Let's speak Italian!** Speaking practice for you
✓ Check your progress with the **CD**

The story

Gary Albergo? Me English. Buono albergo here, close by. Molto economico, but cash only, no carta di credito. Where's there a Bancomat? No idea. Sorry, must dash. Ciao.

Paul Non abbiamo contanti, e con cinque birre non posso andare in macchina. Dov'è il cellulare? Chiamiamo un albergo.

Today's new words

la carta di credito	*the credit card*
un Bancomat	*a cash dispenser*
contanti	*cash*
il cellulare	*the mobile phone*
chiamare, chiamiamo	*to call, let's call*

Today's new sentences

Non posso andare in macchina. Non c'è un Bancomat. Non ho contanti. E dov'è il cellulare? Non posso chiamare l'albergo. Uffa!

NUTS AND BOLTS

potere *can, be able to*
Another essential verb, but you are halfway there already. You already know **posso** *I can* and **possiamo** *we can*. So all that's left to learn is **può** *you can, he/she/it can* and **possono** *they can*. It's all in the **Traveller's companion**.

And just like with **volere** *want* you can attach **potere** to another verb:

Voglio andare – posso andare.	*I want to go – I can go.*
Vogliamo comprare – possiamo comprare.	*We want to buy – we can buy.*
Può andare?	*Can you/he/she/it go?*
Possono comprare una casa in Toscana?	*Can they buy a house in Tuscany?*

No problem!

LET'S SPEAK ITALIAN!

1 Say in Italian:

▶ If I want to, I can buy a glass of wine.
▶ If you want to, you can buy a house.
▶ If we want to, we can buy a car.
▶ If Antonio wants to, he can go on holiday.
▶ If Isabella wants to, she can call a taxi.
▶ If they want to, they can see the hotel.

If you found this exercise a little difficult do it again – fast.

2 Read these sentences OUT LOUD and then answer in Italian, saying 'no':

▶ Possiamo comprare un cellulare?
▶ Posso andare a Genova adesso?
▶ Possiamo fare spese con Antonio?
▶ Posso chiamare l'albergo fra due ore?
▶ Possiamo cercare un autobus per Firenze?
▶ Possono andare in vacanza con Luigi e Chiara?

Day 6

WHAT TO DO TODAY

✓ Read today's five **New words**
✓ Read and work out the **Story** and the **New sentences**
✓ Listen to and speak along with the **CD**
✓ **Nuts and bolts:** Listen to the **CD,** then read and learn them
✓ Learn today's five **New words** and the **New sentences** by heart
✓ Take out the **Traveller's companion.** It's time for another useful verb. Learn **lavorare** *to work.* Then turn back and have a look at the **days of the week**
✓ **Let's speak Italian!** Over to you
✓ Check your progress with the **CD**

The story

Claire C'è un Hotel Palazzo qui a Firenze. Mi piacciono i palazzi.

Paul *(Phoning)* Pronto. Hotel Palazzo? Buongiorno. Ha una camera per due per una notte? … Sì, per oggi … Quanto costa? Cosa? Scusi, CHE COSA? Mmmm …, beh …, grazie. Mamma mia! Non voglio *comprare* il palazzo!

Today's new words

il palazzo	*the palace*
mi piacciono	*I like (more than one thing)*
una camera	*a room*
quanto costa?	*how much does it cost?*
(che) cosa?	*what?*

Today's new sentences

Mi piacciono gli alberghi qui in Toscana. Ecco l'albergo Michelangelo. Va bene? Quanto costa? Beh … no, non mi piace. Che cosa vuole? Una camera in un palazzo?

NUTS AND BOLTS

Mi piacciono le Ferrari
You use **mi piace** if you like *one* thing.

> **Mi piace la mia macchina.**   *I like my car.*

You use **mi piacciono** if you like *more than one* thing.

> **Mi piacciono le Ferrari.**   *I like Ferrari cars.*

LET'S SPEAK ITALIAN!

1 Question time: **che? quando? quanto costa? come?**

Ask in Italian, then answer in Italian – in whole sentences – using the words in brackets.

- ▸ What is Claire looking for? (l'albergo Jolly)
- ▸ When do you want to go to Venice – today or tomorrow? (oggi!)
- ▸ How much is a room? (cento euro per due)
- ▸ How is the centre of Florence? (fantastico!)

2 Here's someone who doesn't like *anything* and says so! Say all the words in Italian starting each time with **Non mi piacciono**.

… the rooms, the questions, the trains, the tickets, the appointments and the bathrooms.

3 A bit of work for every day … Say in Italian:

I work on Monday, you work on Tuesday, does Paolo work on Wednesday? Maria works on Thursday, we work on Friday, they work on Saturday, and … I don't work on Sunday.

Note: In Italian you say **Lavoro il lunedì** *I work the Monday.*

Day 7

◄) CD2, TR 8

Today you are going to mark up your **Progress chart** and see how well you are doing. But first there's a little work to be done ...

WHAT TO DO TODAY

✓ Read the whole **Story** OUT LOUD. You can listen to it by going back to the individual days
✓ Do the four speaking exercises and work out your score

Here's the week's whole story ...

Paul	Vorrei andare a Verona o a Firenze per una notte.
Claire	Andiamo a Firenze. Vorrei vedere gli Uffizi. Come andiamo? In macchina, in autobus o c'è un treno? E ... quando?
Paul	Se andiamo oggi, possiamo andare in macchina. Perché oggi Carlo non ha bisogno della macchina.
Claire	Andiamo oggi!

(After visiting the Uffizi, Paul and Claire are in need of refreshments ...)

Paul	Firenze è fantastica. Mi piace molto. Ma mi piace anche la birra ...
Claire	Per me un bicchiere di vino bianco e ... il bagno.

(Several drinks later they are looking for a hotel. Let's ask someone ...)

	Adesso dobbiamo cercare un albergo. *(Turning to a stranger)* Scusi, può aiutarmi per favore? Cerchiamo un albergo.
Gary	Albergo? Me English. Buono albergo here, close by. Molto economico, but cash only, no carta di credito. Where's there a Bancomat? No idea. Sorry, must dash. Ciao.
Paul	Non abbiamo contanti, e con cinque birre non posso andare in macchina. Dov'è il cellulare? Chiamiamo un albergo.

Claire	C'è un Hotel Palazzo qui a Firenze. Mi piacciono i palazzi.
Paul	*(Phoning)* Pronto. Hotel Palazzo? Buongiorno, Ha una camera per due per una notte? ... Sì, per oggi ... Quanto costa? Cosa? Scusi, CHE COSA? Mmmm ..., beh ..., grazie. Mamma mia! Non voglio *comprare* il palazzo!

AND NOW FOR THE TALKING!

All these are speaking exercises. If you really must write things down, don't do so *until* you have said everything OUT LOUD.

TELL ME, TELL ME ...

... that you would like to see Padova and Vicenza, you can go by train or by car because your friend has a Ferrari and he does not need the car in July. Tell me you would like to see the Uffizi in Florence and that you want to see the hotels in Tuscany. Tell me you like the white wines of Tuscany but you also like the Italian beer (**la birra italiana**). Tell me you must look for a hotel or you can call your friend in Florence with your mobile phone; perhaps he has a room for a night.

Give yourself between ten and 25 points depending on how well you can say it all.

TELL ME IN A FLASH

With the English side facing you, say the **Flash sentences** in Italian. And then check. Give yourself four points for every correct sentence. Take one point off for every mistake.

SPEAK IN ITALIAN!

Practise **dovere** *have to* and **potere** *can*.

▶ I don't have to do the shopping now. I can go home.
▶ You don't have to buy the mobile phone. But you can if you want to.

- We don't have to go on holiday for seven nights. We can go for three.
- They don't have to buy the red wine. They can buy the white.
- He doesn't have to look for the **Bancomat**. He can buy the tickets with the credit card.

Give yourself five points for every correct pair of sentences. Deduct a point for each mistake.

HOW'S YOUR MEMORY?

Now try to remember ... and say the words OUT LOUD.
(Then you can write them down if you wish.)

- Five colours, like **rosa**
- Five verbs in their basic form, like **essere** *to be*
- Five nouns, like **la macchina**
- Five names of months, like **maggio**
- Five days of the week, like **lunedì**
- Five words that have any connection with travelling, like **camera.**

Give yourself one point for each word you remember. Now listen to the **CD** to find out how well you have done.

YOUR RESULT THIS WEEK

Now add up all your points:
- ✓ Tell me, tell me ...   /25
- ✓ Tell me in a flash   /20
- ✓ Speak in Italian!   /25
- ✓ How's your memory?   /30

Total score   **/100%**   **Date** _____

Are you pleased? Don't forget to mark up your **Progress chart**.

Week 5

....

Alla pizzeria
At the pizzeria

The story continues …
* When Claire goes to the supermarket she bumps into old friends,
  Tom and Kate. Later that evening they all go out for a pizza.
  Emilio is their waiter, and he's got a problem …

Day 1

WHAT TO DO TODAY

✓ Read today's five **New words**
✓ Read and work out the **Story** and the **New sentences**
✓ Listen to and speak along with the **CD**
✓ **Nuts and bolts**: Listen to the **CD**, then read and learn them
✓ Look at the **Traveller's companion**. There are lots of useful examples of **verbs in the past tense**
✓ Learn today's five **New words** and the **New sentences** by heart
✓ Test yourself with **Let's speak Italian!** Do the speaking exercise
✓ Check your progress with the **CD**

The story

Claire   Paul, una cosa molto importante: sono stata al supermercato a comprare più vino e ho visto due amici – Tom e Kate!

Today's new words

importante	*important*
sono stato, sono stata	*I have been, I was*
più, di più	*more*
il supermercato	*the supermarket*
ho visto	*I have seen, I saw*

Today's new sentences

Oggi sono stata al supermercato. Ho visto qualcosa che mi piace molto. Un buon vino? No, qualcosa di più importante!

NUTS AND BOLTS

The present and the past
Spot the difference:

> I see two friends.
> I have seen two friends.

The first sentence is happening now.

> **Vedo due amici.**   *I see two friends.*

The second one happened before – or in the past. Claire has been to the supermarket and says:

> **Ho visto due amici.**   *I have seen two friends/I saw two friends.*

When you want to say that you did or have done something, you use **avere** *plus* a form of the 'action' word, the one that describes what you did. For example:

> **Ho visto.**   *I have seen.*

As you already know, we say **ho, ha, abbiamo** or **hanno**, depending on who is doing the action. But – and here's the good news – **visto**, the 'action word', never changes! Here are more examples:

Ho visto la macchina.	*I have seen/I saw* the car.
Ha visto la casa.	*You have seen/You saw* the house.
Ha visto i biglietti.	*He/She has seen/He/She saw* the tickets.
Abbiamo visto il cellulare.	*We have seen/We saw* the mobile phone.
Hanno visto l'albergo.	*They have seen/They saw* the hotel.

Here are two more examples of verbs in the past:

comprare *buy* → **comprato** *bought*
cercare *look for* → **cercato** *looked for*

Now add **ho, ha, abbiamo** or **hanno** and you can say:

Abbiamo comprato la casa.   *We have bought/We bought the house.*
Ho cercato i biglietti.   *I have looked/I looked for the tickets.*

LET'S SPEAK ITALIAN!

Practise the past: **visto, comprato** and **cercato**. Say in Italian:

▶ Did you see the red car at the hotel?
▶ He saw a cheap wine at the supermarket.
▶ I bought more Italian beer because I like it.
▶ They bought four tickets for the train.
▶ We looked for an important palace in Venice.

Day 2

WHAT TO DO TODAY

✓ Read today's five **New words**
✓ Read and work out the **Story** and the **New sentences**
✓ Listen to and speak along with the **CD**
✓ **Nuts and bolts:** Listen to the **CD**, then read and learn them
✓ Look at the **Traveller's companion**. It's time for a few more numbers. Have a look at the **numbers 11–50**
✓ Learn today's five **New words** and the **New sentences** by heart
✓ **Let's speak Italian!** Over to you, and – always speak OUT LOUD
✓ Check your progress with the **CD**

The story
Claire   Siamo andati in un bar e Tom ha detto che hanno visto un appartamento fantastico. Ma Kate non lo vuole. L'appartamento costa molto.

Today's new words

siamo andati	*we have gone, we went*
ha detto	*he/she has said, he/she said*
che	*that*
hanno visto	*they have seen, they saw*
lo	*it*

Today's new sentences
Siamo andati a Roma. Mario ha detto che il Colosseo è fantastico.
Ma non l'ho visto.

NUTS AND BOLTS

Back to the past

… And a bit of bad news … When Claire said **Sono stata al supermercato … siamo andati in un bar** she was talking about something that happened in the past. But this time she actually said *I am been, we are gone*. When you talk about something that involves movement to or from a place, like **andare** *go*, **arrivare** *arrive* or **venire** *come* you form the past with **sono, è, siamo** plus the special form of the 'action' word, the one that describes what you did. You do this also with the verb **essere** *be*. Here are four examples:

sono andato/a	*I have gone*
è arrivato/a	*you have arrived*
	he/she/it has arrived
siamo stati/e	*we have been*
sono venuti/e	*they have come*

Unfortunately this time the endings of the second verb can change too, depending on WHO has done it – male or female, one person or more.

If this is getting all too much stop right here! Listen to it on the **CD** and then try the exercise in **Let's speak Italian!** You'll realize it's not that complicated.

It and *them*

Kate non lo vuole.	*Kate does not want it.*
	(l'appartamento)

Imagine you are talking about things such as *wine*, *the house*, *the tickets* or *the cars*. Now imagine you are referring to these things. You would say *it* or *them*. In Italian *it* is **lo** or **la**, and *them* is **li** or **le**, depending if the things you are referring to are masculine or feminine, one thing or more.

Compro il vino, lo compro.	*I buy it.*
Compra la casa, la compra.	*You buy it.*
Ha i biglietti a casa, li ha a casa.	*He has them at home.*
Abbiamo le macchine in blu, le abbiamo in blu.	*We have them in blue.*

Did you notice? The *it* or *them* always goes in front of the verb. For example, if you talk about buying *a ticket* **un biglietto,** or two **due biglietti,** you would say: *It I buy.* **Lo compro.** *Them I buy.* **Li compro.**

Got it? Listen to it once more on the **CD.**

LET'S SPEAK ITALIAN!

1 Practise **detto** *said* and **stato, stata, stati, state** *gone*.

Say in Italian:

▶ I said that he has gone to the flat.
▶ He said that Luigi and Roberto have gone to Italy.
▶ You said that you have gone home.
▶ We said that she has gone to the supermarket.
▶ She said that I have gone to the bar.
▶ Did you say that I have gone to the station?
▶ I did not say that you (Lara) have gone home. Maria said it.

2 Here are some prices. They are all in euros. Say them.

€6.01: **sei euro e un centesimo**
€15.50: **quindici euro e cinquanta centesimi**

If you are getting a mouth full of teeth trying to say this – relax! When the euros are followed by a big number of **centesimi,** for example 50 **cinquanta** or 75 **settantacinque,** the word **centesimo** is usually dropped.

€3.50: **tre euro e cinquanta**

Now you. Say these euros in Italian:

€30.10, €3.25, €10.46, €52.04

3 Read the Italian sentences out loud. Then replace the words in **bold type** with the Italian for *it* or *them*, and say the sentence. For example:

Compro **un cappuccino**. *I buy it.* Lo compro.

▶ Vuole **una birra**? *Do you want it?*
▶ Compriamo **un appartamento**? *Are we buying it?*
▶ Cerca **l'autobus**? *Are you looking for it?*
▶ Paola ha visto **il treno** alla stazione. *She has seen it.*
▶ Cercano due **camere**. *They are looking for them.*

Day 3

WHAT TO DO TODAY

An easy day!

- ✓ Read today's five **New words**
- ✓ Read and work out the **Story** and the **New sentences**
- ✓ Listen to and speak along with the **CD**
- ✓ Learn today's five **New words** and the **New sentences** by heart
- ✓ **Nuts and bolts:** Listen to the **CD,** then read and learn them
- ✓ **Let's speak Italian!** Only one exercise today
- ✓ Check your progress with the **CD**

The story

Paul Perché non andiamo a mangiare con loro? Mi piacciono Tom e Kate. Possiamo andare in un ristorante, o meglio, in una pizzeria. Hanno il cellulare? Chiamiamo Tom e Kate!

Claire Sì, li chiamo.

Today's new words

perché	*why*
mangiare	*eat, to eat*
loro	*they, them*
un ristorante	*a restaurant*
meglio	*better*

Today's new sentences

Perché non vuole andare al ristorante con Gianni e Maria? Perché loro non mi piacciono. Perché non vuole mangiare le pizze? Perché sono care.

NUTS AND BOLTS

More on the past

Remember **lo, la, li** and **le** *it* and *them*? Put them right in front of the *whole* verb. For example:

She called the hotel.	**Ha chiamato l'albergo.**
She called it.	**Lo ha chiamato.**
	or better, contracted:
	L'ha chiamato.

But what happens if she has called *the girlfriend*, has bought *the tickets*, or looked for *the houses*? If we want to say she has called *her* (the girlfriend), has bought *them* (the tickets) or looked for *them* (the houses) the end of the second verb must 'rhyme along', in other words follow the **la, li** and **le**. Here are all four examples:

alberg**o**	**lo** ha (l'ha) chiamat**o**
amic**a**	**la** ha (l'ha) chiamat**a**
bigliett**i**	**li** ha comprat**i**
cas**e**	l'**e** ha cercat**e**

LET'S SPEAK ITALIAN!

Say in Italian and practise *it* and *them* with **chiamato** *called*.

- ▶ I called the restaurant. I called it.
- ▶ Did you call the bank for me? Did you call it for me?
- ▶ She has called two friends today. She has called them today.
- ▶ Did you call the mobile on Monday? Did you call it on Monday?
- ▶ They called the three stations in Rome. They called them in Rome.
- ▶ She called four restaurants in London. She called them in London.

You may have found this difficult at first. Just do it once more. And here's a bit of good news: it doesn't get harder than this. On the contrary!

Day 4

WHAT TO DO TODAY

✓ Read today's five **New words**
✓ Read and work out the **Story** and the **New sentences**
✓ Look at the **Traveller's companion.** You'll find some useful words about **eating and drinking**
✓ Listen to and speak along with the **CD**
✓ Learn today's five **New words** and the **New sentences** by heart
✓ **Let's speak Italian!** You're going to take charge in the restaurant!
✓ Check your progress with the **CD**

The story
(Alla pizzeria)

Paul   Cosa mangiamo?

Kate   Per me la pizza 'Roma' e … da bere … un'acqua minerale.

Tom   Lo stesso per me, e una bottiglia di vino bianco.

Claire Mi piacciono gli spaghetti. E da bere … una birra e un'acqua frizzante.

Paul   Per me una pizza napoletana e una birra.

Today's new words

bere, da bere	*to drink*
acqua minerale	*mineral water*
lo stesso	*the same*
una bottiglia	*a bottle*
acqua frizzante	*sparkling water*

Today's new sentences
Da mangiare – una pizza, per favore.
Da bere – una bottiglia di vino rosso della casa.
E per Lei? Lo stesso, per favore.

LET'S SPEAK ITALIAN!

1 **Da mangiare? Da bere?** Pretend you are having dinner with five friends in a restaurant. You have to order for everyone at your table. Use the words you have learned plus some of the ones in the **Traveller's companion**. Here's an example:

> Il pollo alla griglia, per favore con patate fritte, e da bere un bicchiere di vino bianco.

Now order for your five friends in the same way. First the food and then **e da bere** .... You can have the **Traveller's companion** open to help you along.

2 Memory test: I have picked four **New words** from every week you have done so far – that's a total of 20. Let's see how many you remember. Say them and then check them yourself.

> but, how, broken, the sun, perhaps, two hours, the bill, on the right, my, a question, good, also, to see, a night, cash, now, better, that, more, why?

Day 5

WHAT TO DO TODAY

✓ Read today's five **New words**
✓ Read and work out the **Story** and the **New sentences**
✓ Listen to and speak along with the **CD**
✓ Learn today's five **New words** and the **New sentences** by heart
✓ **Let's speak Italian!** Just one short exercise today
✓ Check your progress with the **CD**

> **The story**
> *(Later)*
> **Emilio** *(The waiter)* Ecco il conto!
> **Tom** Il conto è per me.
> **Paul** No, no, per favore, il conto è *per me*. Claire, dov'è la mia carta di credito? Non ce l'ho.
> **Claire** È a casa.
> **Paul** Questo è terribile! Mi dispiace, Tom, non ho la mia carta e non ho contanti. Solo tre euro.

Today's new words

non ce l'ho	*I don't have it*
credo che ...	*I believe that ..., I think that ...*
questo	*this*
terribile	*terrible*
solo	*only*

Today's new sentences

Questo non mi piace. C'è il tiramisù. Il tiramisù? No, non ce l'abbiamo. Beh. Solo un tè per me. Mamma mia! Il tè è terribile.

LET'S SPEAK ITALIAN!

Make up five sentences using the words in brackets. Start every
sentence with **Credo che ...**

▶ Credo che ... (Italia, agosto, solo, siamo, per)
▶   (abbiamo, carta di credito, questo, comprato)
▶   (visto, lo, supermercato, abbiamo, a destra)
▶   (qui, non, siamo, a casa, oggi)

Day 6

WHAT TO DO TODAY

✓ Read today's five **New words**
✓ Read and work out the **Story** and the **New sentences**
✓ Look at the **Traveller's companion.** You'll find some interesting **sample menus,** for breakfast, lunch and dinner
✓ Listen to and speak along with the **CD**
✓ Learn today's five **New words** and the **New sentences** by heart
✓ **Let's speak Italian!** More speaking practice for you
✓ Check your progress with the **CD**

The story

Tom   Paul, per favore! Non è un gran conto. Dov'è il cameriere? Ha la mia carta.

Emilio Ho un problema – perchélacartaèrotta.

Tom   Che cosa c'è? Un problema? Non è possibile. Che problema? Può parlare più lentamente, per favore?

Emilio Ho – un – problema – perché – la carta – è – rotta.

Today's new words

grande, gran	*big*
il cameriere	*the waiter*
che cosa c'è?	*what's the matter?*
possibile	*possible*
può parlare più lentamente?	*can you speak more slowly?*

Today's new sentences

Che cosa c'è? Chiamo da (*from*) Londra. Può parlare più lentamente per favore? Un gran problema? Cosa? Questo non è possibile!

LET'S SPEAK ITALIAN!

1 Warm up with the five **Flash sentences** for this week. Did you 'turn and learn'? Test yourself – speaking OUT LOUD – until you are word perfect.

2 Something has happened. Something is wrong. You don't know what, so you ask: **Che cosa c'è?** Here's what happened – for you to say in Italian. Ask first *What's the matter?* and then reply.

▶ The restaurant is terrible. They don't have wine, only beer.
▶ I have not seen the bus, and I have to go to an appointment.
▶ My mobile phone is broken. Can you please speak more slowly?
▶ I have a problem: the bill is large and I don't have a credit card.
▶ I think this is not possible: six euros for a glass of house wine?

3 Now for more food and drink ... Pretend you are out with your partner, for breakfast, lunch and dinner. After consulting the **Traveller's companion**, order two breakfasts, two lunches and two dinners. Place your orders speaking OUT LOUD!

Day 7

Today you receive your reward for all the learning you've done during this week: a great result on your **Progress chart!** But first there's a little work to be done...

WHAT TO DO TODAY

✓ Read the whole **Story** OUT LOUD
✓ Do the oral exercises which follow the **Story** and score up to 100%!

....
Here is this week's whole story ...

Claire   Paul, una cosa molto importante: sono stata al supermercato a comprare più vino e ho visto due amici – Tom e Kate! Siamo andati in un bar e Tom ha detto che hanno visto un appartamento fantastico. Ma Kate non lo vuole. L'appartamento costa molto.

Paul   Perché non andiamo a mangiare con loro? Mi piacciono Tom e Kate. Possiamo andare in un ristorante, o meglio, in una pizzeria. Hanno il cellulare? Chiamiamo Tom e Kate.

Claire   Sì, li chiamo.
(Alla pizzeria)

Paul   Cosa mangiamo?

Kate   Per me la pizza 'Roma' e ... da bere ... un'acqua minerale.

Tom   Lo stesso per me, e una bottiglia di vino bianco.

Claire   Mi piacciono gli spaghetti. E da bere ... una birra e un'acqua frizzante.

Paul   Per me una pizza napoletana e una birra.
(Later)

Emilio   *(The waiter)* Ecco il conto!

Tom   Il conto è per me.

(Contd)
....

Paul	No, no, per favore, il conto è *per me*. Claire, dov'è la mia carta di credito? Non ce l'ho.
Claire	È a casa.
Paul	Questo è terribile! Mi dispiace, Tom, non ho la mia carta e non ho contanti. Solo tre euro.
Tom	Paul, per favore! Non è un gran conto. Dov'è il cameriere? Ha la mia carta.
Emilio	Ho un problema – perchélacartaèrotta.
Tom	Che cosa c'è? Un problema? Non è possibile. Che problema? Può parlare più lentamente, per favore?
Emilio	Ho – un – problema – perché – la carta – è – rotta.

TELL ME, TELL ME – IN THE PAST!

… that you went to the supermarket today, that you saw a lot of people in the supermarket, that you bought water, beer and wine, that you went by car and that you saw Anna, a friend … that Anna saw your car at the cafeteria of the supermarket … that Anna said: 'Let's go and eat a pizza' and that you (*you two, girls*) went to a restaurant … that the bill was (**era**) very large and that Anna said: 'Mamma mia' and that after (**dopo**) two bottles of wine you went home by taxi.

REMEMBER YOUR WORDS?

▶ Take out all the **Flash cards** for Weeks 3 and 4 – 30 for each week. Out of each 30 pick out 15 at random.
▶ With the English facing you test yourself, saying the Italian OUT LOUD. Check after each word.
▶ Put the correct cards on one side and the ones you got wrong or did not know on the other. Give yourself a point for each one you got right.
▶ Have a quick look at the ones you did not know. Spend five minutes on these.

REMEMBER THE STORY?

Answer these questions in Italian – OUT LOUD!

- ▶ Dov'è stata Claire?
- ▶ Perché è andata al supermercato?
- ▶ Dov'è andata con gli amici?
- ▶ Che cosa ha detto Tom?
- ▶ Perché Kate non vuole comprare l'appartamento?
- ▶ Dove vanno i quattro amici?
- ▶ Che cosa vuole mangiare Claire?
- ▶ Che cosa vuole bere Tom?
- ▶ Che cosa è terribile?
- ▶ Il cameriere che problema ha?

If you struggled through this exercise give yourself 10 points, if you marched through it make it 20. And if you raced through it give yourself 25 points.

SPEAK IN ITALIAN!

- ▶ Say ten numbers between 11 and 50.
- ▶ Give ten items you may find on a menu.
- ▶ After you've said them write them down and check them in the **Traveller's companion**. Score up to 20 points.

YOUR RESULT THIS WEEK

- ✓ Tell me, tell me … in the past!   /25
- ✓ Remember your words?   /30
- ✓ Remember the story?   /25
- ✓ Speak in Italian!   /20

Total score   **/100%**   **Date** _____

Depending on your score you can either pat yourself on the back, wring your hands or … do it again!

Don't forget to enter your result on the **Progress chart**.

Week 6

··

Devo andare dal medico
I must go to the doctor's

The story continues ...

- *Paul is not feeling well. Too much sun? Too much to drink? Too much spaghetti with hot arrabbiata sauce? Too many seafood cocktails? Claire phones for a medical appointment. When they get to the surgery late and the doctor has gone Paul makes a remarkable recovery ...*

Day 1

WHAT TO DO TODAY

✓ Read the five **New words**
✓ Read and work out the **Story** and the **New sentences**
✓ Listen to and speak along with the **CD**
✓ Learn today's five **New words** and the **New sentences**
   by heart
✓ Test yourself with **Let's speak Italian!**
✓ Check your progress with the **CD**

The story

Paul   Ho bisogno del medico. Non posso mangiare. Non posso
            bere, solo tè. Non so che cos'è.

Claire Oh! Mi dispiace. Sì, abbiamo bisogno del medico.
            (On the phone to the surgery) Pronto, buongiorno, vorrei
            un appuntamento. Sì, per oggi. A che ora? … Non prima?
            … Va bene … Sì, grazie. Il nome? È Blair, signor Blair,
            B-l-a-i-r. Sì, come Tony.

Today's new words

il medico, dal medico	*the doctor, to the doctor's*
il tè	*the tea*
non so, non lo so	*I don't know, I don't know it*
prima	*before*
come	*like*

Today's new sentences

Voglio un appuntamento con il medico. Quando? Non so … forse alle
quattro? Alle sette? Non prima? Il mio nome? Sono Peggy Thatcher.
Sì, come Margaret.

LET'S SPEAK ITALIAN!

1 Say these sentences in Italian.

▶ I don't know where the supermarket is.
▶ I am sorry, I don't know it.
▶ What does he want to eat? I know (it) …
▶ I don't know how much the appointment with the doctor costs.
▶ I don't know if I like the red wine.

2 Complete the sentences. Use these phrases (in Italian!). Speak OUT LOUD!

in September, Milan is bigger, he has gone shopping, there is only coffee, the doctor is not here

▶ Dov'è il medico? Non lo so, forse …
▶ C'è un appuntamento con il medico prima delle undici? Non lo so perché …
▶ Quando va in vacanza? Non lo so. Forse …
▶ È grande Manchester? Come Milano? Non lo so, ma forse …
▶ Mi piace il tè, ma oggi …

Day 2

WHAT TO DO TODAY

✓ Read the five **New words**
✓ Read and work out the **Story** and the **New sentences**
✓ **About time … and the weather!** This is a section in the **Traveller's companion**. Have a look at it
✓ Listen to and speak along with the **CD**
✓ Learn today's five **New words** and the **New sentences** by heart
✓ **Let's speak Italian!** Two easy speaking exercises
✓ Check your progress with the **CD**

The story

Claire	Abbiamo un appuntamento col medico alle due. Adesso sono le undici.
Paul	Voglio andare ai negozi e ho bisogno della banca. Abbiamo tre ore per tutto. È sufficiente. Ma non so a che ora è aperta la banca.

Today's new words

il negozio, i negozi	*the shop, the shops*
la banca	*the bank*
tutto	*all, everything*
sufficiente	*sufficient, enough*
aperto, aperta	*open*

Today's new sentences

Tutti i negozi sono aperti. Quanti euro abbiamo? È sufficiente o abbiamo bisogno della banca?

LET'S SPEAK ITALIAN!

1 Complete these questions to fit the answers.

▶ Quando ...?

Answer: Devo andare ai negozi alle nove.

▶ Perché ...?

Answer: Perché costa molto mangiare in un ristorante.

▶ Quanto costano ...?

Answer: I sei bicchieri gialli costano dodici euro.

▶ È aperto ...?

Answer: No, non è aperto la domenica.

▶ Che cosa ...?

Answer: Voglio comprare tutto! Beh ... voglio comprare una bottiglia di acqua.

2 **Telling the time.** Have another look at the **Traveller's companion** to help you. Now say in Italian:

▶ What time is it?   At what time are we going?
▶ It is half past three.   We are going at half past three.
▶ It is five o'clock.   We are going at five o'clock.
▶ It is a quarter to nine.   We are going at a quarter to nine in the evening.
▶ It is a quarter past seven. We are going at a quarter past seven in the morning.
▶ It is one o'clock.   We are going at one o'clock.

Day 3

● **CD2, TR 18**

WHAT TO DO TODAY

✓ Read the five **New words**
✓ Read and work out the **Story** and the **New sentences**
✓ Take out the **Traveller's companion**. You'll find some
  everyday adjectives. Have a read through
✓ Listen to and speak along with the **CD**
✓ Learn today's five **New words** and the **New sentences** by heart
✓ **Let's speak Italian!** Two easy speaking exercises
✓ Check your progress with the **CD**

The story
(Later)

Paul   Cerco un negozio vicino alla via principale e vicino alla
           banca. Ho bisogno di qualcosa per la macchina di Carlo.
           Costa meno laggiù.

Today's new words

cerco	*I am looking for*
vicino, vicino a	*near, near to*
la via/strada principale	*the main street/road*
meno	*less*
là, laggiù	*there, down there*

Today's new sentences

Cerco una pizzeria qui vicino, nella via principale. Le pizze sono
buone e costano meno laggiù.

LET'S SPEAK ITALIAN!

1 Make up eight sentences with **cerco** … and carry on with **perché voglio** … Use the items in the lists below, choosing one from List A to go with one from List B. Here's an example:

Cerco un bar, perché voglio un brandy.

Make sure you say your sentences OUT LOUD!

List A

un'agenzia di viaggio, un medico, un cameriere, un albergo, una via principale, un Bancomat, un treno, la strada per il mare

List B

una camera per una notte, un appuntamento per domani, vedere un appartamento laggiù, andare a Bari, più soldi, andare in vacanza, il conto, un autobus per il centro

2 Say these sentences in Italian. They include ten everyday adjectives from the **Traveller's companion**.

▶ It is difficult to do everything. First I must go to the doctor's and then …
▶ It is an old house and always dirty.
▶ It is a fast car and dangerous.
▶ Maria is likeable and very kind.
▶ It is stupid to drink ten glasses of wine but it is not forbidden.

Day 4

WHAT TO DO TODAY

- ✓ Read the five **New words**
- ✓ Read and work out the **Story** and the **New sentences**
- ✓ **I am ill!** Consult the **Traveller's companion** to get help.
  Have a read through
- ✓ Listen to and speak along with the **CD**
- ✓ Learn today's five **New words** and the **New sentences** by heart
- ✓ **Let's speak Italian!** Two easy speaking exercises
- ✓ Check your progress with the **CD**

The story

Claire Ma la macchina va bene, no? L'altro giorno Carlo ha lavorato con la macchina fino alle dieci di sera.

Paul Sì, ma non è una macchina nuova ... È una macchina terribile!

Today's new words

va bene	*it's all right*
l'altro	*the other (one)*
ha lavorato	*he has worked, he worked*
fino a	*until*
nuovo, nuova	*new*

Today's new sentences

Ha lavorato nel nuovo negozio fino alle undici di notte. Non va bene. Perché non lavora in un altro negozio?

LET'S SPEAK ITALIAN!

1 Say in Italian – OUT LOUD!

▶ The car is new and it's cheap but I don't want it.
▶ They are at home until nine o'clock in the evening.
▶ I like it but the other one is less expensive.
▶ Is it all right if I eat everything?
▶ Did he work or didn't he work? I don't know.

2 Doctor, doctor … Complete these sentences with the words in brackets.

▶ Vorrei qualcosa per (*stomach pains*).
▶ Ho (*a backache*).
▶ Devo andare (*to the chemist's*).
▶ Ha qualcosa (*for a headache*)?
▶ Ho (*the tablets*) e adesso ho bisogno di (*an invoice and a receipt*).

Day 5

◀️ **CD2, TR 20**

WHAT TO DO TODAY

- ✓ Read the five **New words**
- ✓ Read and work out the **Story** and the **New sentences**
- ✓ More numbers: they are in the **Traveller's companion.** Have a look at **numbers 50 to 1,000**
- ✓ Listen to and speak along with the **CD**
- ✓ Learn today's five **New words** and the **New sentences** by heart
- ✓ **Let's speak Italian!** Two easy speaking exercises
- ✓ Check your progress with the **CD**

The story
(Più tardi)

Claire Abbiamo comprato molte cose e … un piccolo cellulare molto caro. Paul, adesso abbiamo cinque cellulari!

Paul Non è caro. Non è niente. Costa troppo in Inghilterra. Adesso abbiamo bisogno di andare dal medico. Dov'è?

Claire Non lo so, forse è in via Vivaldi, molto vicino.

Today's new words

più tardi	*later*
una cosa, le cose	*a thing, the things*
piccolo	*little, small*
niente	*nothing*
troppo	*too, too much*

Today's new sentences

Non c'è niente in casa! Più tardi siamo stati a un supermercato in via Fellini. Abbiamo cercato qualcosa da mangiare, e … abbiamo comprato troppo! Il supermercato è piccolo ma ha molte cose economiche.

LET'S SPEAK ITALIAN!

1 Complete these sentences with the help of the words in brackets. Are you still speaking OUT LOUD? I am listening!

▶ Ho comprato (*small car*) ma (*now don't like it*).
▶ Abbiamo visto (*supermarket*) e più tardi (*gone shopping*).
▶ Abbiamo detto a (*estate agency*) que (*looking for flat, but not too big*).
▶ Siamo andati (*Rome, eight o'clock in the morning*) e più tardi (*bought many things*).
▶ Sono stato/a (*at doctor*) ma (*have nothing*).

2 More numbers. Say these in Italian. You can use the **Traveller's companion** to help you. Say them twice with help, and then try once more without looking.

66, 75, 97, 350, 500, 620, 844, 1000

Day 6

🔊 **CD2, TR 21**

WHAT TO DO TODAY

✓ Read the five **New words**
✓ Read and work out the **Story** and the **New sentences**
✓ Listen to and speak along with the **CD**
✓ Learn today's five **New words** and the **New sentences** by heart
✓ **Let's speak Italian!** One quick exercise and one that's a little longer …
✓ Check your progress with the **CD**

The story
(At the surgery)

Claire   È qui, numero trentadue.

Paul   Buongiorno. Sono Paul Blair. Ho un appuntamento col medico. Alle due.

Marta   *(The receptionist)* Mi dispiace. L'appuntamento era alle dodici, non alle due.

Claire   Non capisco. Alle dodici?

Marta   Sì. Per oggi non ci sono più appuntamenti. Sono finiti. Il medico è andato a casa. Adesso siamo chiusi.

Paul   Oh, mi dispiace. Beh … andiamo. Buongiorno.

(Nella macchina)

Claire   E cosa facciamo adesso?

Paul   Niente. Non importa. Col nuovo cellulare non ho più bisogno del medico. Andiamo a mangiare. Forse un curry o le penne all'arrabbiata … ?

Today's new words

era, erano	*he/she/it was, they were*
non capisco	*I don't understand*
finito	*finished*
chiuso	*closed*
cosa facciamo?	*what do we do?*

LET'S SPEAK ITALIAN!

1 Say these sentences quickly in Italian.

where is the number? she was from Turin, the shop is closed, the photo is finished, what do we do tomorrow? I don't understand what you want

2 You've been offered the appointments below. Say them OUT LOUD in Italian. Here are two examples:

5th November	**il cinque novembre**
Monday, 5th November	**lunedì cinque novembre**

Did you spot the difference? Yes, you drop **il** when it's a simple date without the day of the week. But nobody will fall about laughing if you get it wrong!

▶ Tuesday, 12 June at 10 p.m.
▶ 22 August at 4 p.m.
▶ Thursday, 3 October at 11 a.m.
▶ Friday, 20 December at 8.30 p.m.
▶ 30 March at 8 a.m.
▶ Sunday, 14 May at 2.45 p.m.

If it took you a long time to work out say it again … in half the time!

Day 7

◀) CD2, TR 22

It's the end of the week. Only one more week to go. Now for the self-assessment.

WHAT TO DO TODAY

✓ Read the whole **Story** OUT LOUD
✓ Then complete the five exercises and score maximum points

Here's this week's whole story ...

Paul Ho bisogno del medico. Non posso mangiare. Non posso bere, solo tè. Non so che cos'è.

Claire Oh! Mi dispiace. Sì, abbiamo bisogno del medico. *(On the phone to the surgery)* Pronto, buongiorno, vorrei un appuntamento. Sì, per oggi. A che ora? ... Non prima? ... Va bene ... Sì, grazie. Il nome? È Blair, signor Blair, B-l-a-i-r. Sì, come Tony. *(To Paul)* Abbiamo un appuntamento col medico alle due. Adesso sono le undici.

Paul Voglio andare ai negozi e ho bisogno della banca. Abbiamo tre ore per tutto. È sufficiente. Ma non so a che ora è aperta la banca.

(Later)

Paul Cerco un negozio vicino alla via principale e vicino alla banca. Ho bisogno di qualcosa per la macchina di Carlo. Costa meno laggiù.

Claire Ma la macchina va bene, no? L'altro giorno Carlo ha lavorato con la macchina fino alle dieci di sera.

Paul Sì, ma non è una macchina nuova ... È una macchina terribile!

(Più tardi)

Claire Abbiamo comprato molte cose e ... un piccolo cellulare molto caro. Paul, adesso abbiamo cinque cellulari!

Paul	Non è caro. Non è niente. Costa troppo in Inghilterra. Adesso abbiamo bisogno di andare dal medico. Dov'è?
Claire	Non lo so, forse è in via Vivaldi, molto vicino.

(At the surgery)

Claire	È qui, numero trentadue.
Paul	Buongiorno. Sono Paul Blair. Ho un appuntamento col medico. Alle due.
Marta	*(The receptionist)* Mi dispiace. L'appuntamento era alle dodici, non alle due.
Claire	Non capisco. Alle dodici?
Marta	Sì. Per oggi non ci sono più appuntamenti. Sono finiti. Il medico è andato a casa. Adesso siamo chiusi.
Paul	Oh, mi dispiace. Beh ... andiamo. Buongiorno.

(Nella macchina)

Claire	E cosa facciamo adesso?
Paul	Niente. Non importa. Col nuovo cellulare non ho più bisogno del medico. Andiamo a mangiare. Forse un curry o le penne all'arrabbiata ... ?

TELL ME, TELL ME...

... that you have a stomach ache (**mal di pancia**), that you do not like it and that you have to go to the doctor's .... that your friend said there is a good doctor from Milan and that he is in the centre of Rimini near the sea in the via Veneto, number 54 ... that you have an appointment today at 9 o'clock in the morning

... that you have been to the doctor and that he was very kind, and that he said it was nothing, only too much wine ... that the bill was not large – only 25 euros – and that afterwards you went to a restaurant for spaghetti with clams and a small glass of white wine.

When you have said the piece OUT LOUD and listened to it on the **CD** give yourself ten points for a fair attempt, 20 for quite good and 25 points for very good.

REMEMBER IN A FLASH

Take out the **Flash sentences** from Weeks 2, 3 and 4, a total of 15 cards. With the English facing you, say the Italian and then check. If you can say the sentence in a flash, give yourself two points for each one. If it takes a little longer or you don't get it quite right, give yourself one point for the sentence.

AT THE PHARMACY

You are planning a weekend in the Abruzzi mountains and are stocking up at the pharmacy – just in case.

- ▶ Say you would like something for a headache.
- ▶ Ask them if they have something for a stomach ache.
- ▶ Tell them you need sun cream (a cream for the sun).
- ▶ Tell them you have a cough, but only at night. Do they have a linctus (**uno sciroppo**)?
- ▶ Tell them you need an invoice and a receipt.
- ▶ Ask them how much it is.
- ▶ Tell them that you are sorry but that you do not have cash.
- ▶ Ask them if a credit card is OK.
- ▶ Ask them if there is a doctor nearby.
- ▶ Say goodbye and thank them for everything.

After saying it all OUT LOUD listen to the **CD** and give yourself between five and 15 points, depending on how well you did.

BONUS ADJECTIVES

Have another five-minute read of the 'bonus' adjectives in the **Traveller's companion**. Read them OUT LOUD to yourself three times. Now close the booklet. How many can you remember and use to describe each of the words below? Here's an example:

il supermercato, il supermercato **pulito**

If you cannot think of a bonus adjective, add one of the familiar ones or even a colour.

> la macchina, il negozio, le cose, il numero, la via, il tè,
> l'appartamento, l'albergo, il cameriere, la bottiglia

A bonus adjective earns you two points, any adjective or colour you have learned earlier earns you one point.

REMEMBER YOUR VERBS

Just to make sure you don't get rusty on your verbs here are ten to remember. Say them in Italian and give yourself one point for each correct one.

> he has worked, I have seen, she wants to drink, he cannot eat,
> I cannot go, she has gone, they buy, you go shopping, I would
> like to call, we are looking for

YOUR RESULT THIS WEEK

✓ Tell me, tell me ...	/25
✓ Remember in a flash	/30
✓ At the pharmacy	/15
✓ Bonus adjectives	/20
✓ Remember your verbs	/10

Total score   **/100%**   **Date** _____

A great result? Record it on the **Progress chart!**

Week 7

Arrivederci Italia ... ma abbiamo le foto!

Goodbye Italy ... but we have the photos!

The story concludes ...

- *It's the end of their holiday with a last minute rush buying presents and taking photos. Then it's off to the airport in Carlo's unreliable car. Will Paul and Claire miss the plane? Will they argue over the photos? And what does Paul have up his sleeve?*

Day 1

WHAT TO DO TODAY

- ✓ Read the five **New words**
- ✓ Read and work out the **Story** and the **New sentences**
- ✓ Have a final look at the **Traveller's companion**. There are some **useful verbs** for 'the inspired' which will come in handy. Browse through them …
- ✓ Listen to and speak along with the **CD**
- ✓ Learn today's five **New words** and the **New sentences** by heart
- ✓ **Let's speak Italian!** Two easy speaking exercises
- ✓ Check your progress with the **CD**

The story

Paul   Non lo credo! È già sabato. Solo più un giorno di vacanza. Che cosa facciamo oggi?

Claire   Voglio comprare qualcosa di bello per il mio direttore – all'Upim.

Today's new words

già	*already*
il giorno	*the day*
bello, bella	*beautiful, handsome, nice*
il direttore	*the boss, manager, director*
Upim	*well-known Italian department store*

Today's new sentences

Sono le quattro. Il direttore è già andato a casa. Non voglio più lavorare. Vorrei andare a comprare qualcosa di bello. Che facciamo? Beh … andiamo!

LET'S SPEAK ITALIAN!

1 Make up five sentences starting with **andiamo!** *let's go* and do something! Finish off with **Va bene!** For example:

Andiamo a cercare un bell'hotel in Toscana! Va bene!

Now you speak. The longer the sentence, the better.

▶ Andiamo a mangiare ...
▶ Andiamo a comprare ...
▶ Andiamo a bere ...
▶ Andiamo a chiamare ...
▶ Andiamo a fare spese ...

2 A few extra verbs from the **Traveller's companion** ... for 'the inspired'.

arrivare – arrivato	*arrive – arrived*
parlare – parlato	*speak – spoken*
venire – venuto	*come – come*
sapere – saputo	*know – known*

and nine easy sentences for you to say in Italian:

▶ I must arrive tomorrow.
▶ He has arrived with his new car.
▶ We would like to speak English (**inglese**).
▶ He did not speak English when he was in Italy.
▶ We must come to the station with them.
▶ She has come with a terrible girlfriend.
▶ I knew that she was pretty.
▶ They want to know if Marco is here.
▶ Do they know that he is at home?

Day 2

WHAT TO DO TODAY

✓ Read the five **New words**
✓ Read and work out the **Story** and the **New sentences**
✓ Listen to and speak along with the **CD**
✓ Learn today's five **New words** and the **New sentences** by heart
✓ **Let's speak Italian!** Two easy speaking exercises
✓ Check your progress with the **CD**

The story

Paul   Voglio fare delle foto – non abbiamo una foto di noi due. Chi può aiutare? C'è qualcuno che …?

Claire   *(Turning to a stranger)* Ah, scusi, può aiutarmi, per favore, a fare una foto? Sì, con mio marito, qui, a tavola.

Today's new words

la foto, fare delle foto	*the photo, to take photos*
noi	*we, us*
chi	*who*
il marito, mio marito	*the husband, my husband*
la tavola	*the table*

Today's new sentences

Mio marito ha fatto (*made, taken*) due foto: una di noi due e l'altra della tavola. Chi ha visto le foto? C'è qualcuno che le ha viste? … Non lo so.

LET'S SPEAK ITALIAN!

1 Who did it? I don't know, but somebody did it. Answer these questions by saying **Non lo so** and replace the word in bold with *it* or *them*. Here's an example:

Chi ha visto **il treno**? Non lo so, ma qualcuno l'ha visto.

Now you try OUT LOUD:

▶ Chi ha fatto **le spese**?
▶ Chi ha chiamato **l'albergo**?
▶ Chi ha comprato **la Ferrari**?
▶ Chi ha detto **questo**?
▶ Chi ha visto **i biglietti**?

It's not easy to say this quickly. But you get faster if you do this exercise a couple of times more.

2 Last round of mental acrobatics. Four more verbs for the inspired:

dare – dato	*give – given*
scrivere – scritto	*write – written*
sperare – sperato	*hope – hoped*
prendere – preso	*take – taken*

and five easy sentences for you to say in Italian:

▶ She wants to give something to Miss Verdi.
▶ He has given all the money to us.
▶ He has written to the director of (the) Upim.
▶ We hope to arrive in Italy in May.
▶ I take the car but I haven't taken the cash.

Day 3

WHAT TO DO TODAY

- ✓ Read the five **New words**
- ✓ Read and work out the **Story** and the **New sentences**
- ✓ Listen to and speak along with the **CD**
- ✓ Learn today's five **New words** and the **New sentences** by heart
- ✓ **Let's speak Italian!** Two easy speaking exercises
- ✓ Check your progress with the **CD**

The story
(The next day)

Claire   È domenica. Arrivederci Italia! Non mi piace andare in Inghilterra. C'è brutto tempo là e lunedì devo lavorare.

Gina   Ma Birmingham è interessante, no?

Carlo   Ecco la mia macchina. Andiamo all'aeroporto. Non abbiamo molto tempo.

Today's new words

brutto	*ugly, bad*
il tempo	*time, weather*
devo lavorare	*I must work*
interessante	*interesting*
l'aeroporto	*the airport*

Today's new sentences
Se devo lavorare, vorrei lavorare in un aeroporto. È interessante e non importa se il tempo è brutto.

LET'S SPEAK ITALIAN!

1 *do you like?* **le piace? le piacciono?**

Look at the examples:

> *Going shopping, do you like it?*
> **Fare spese, le piace?**
> *The shops, do you like them?*
> **I negozi, le piacciono?**

Now ask someone in Italian if he likes:

> The Ferraris, do you like them?
> My mobile phone, do you like it?
> The new supermarket, do you like it?
> The wines from Tuscany, do you like them?

2 If you want to ask if someone *would* like something you use **piacerebbe,** and if it's more than one thing he would like it's **piacerebbero.** Here's an example:

Le piacerebbe mangiare ...? *(a pizza in the restaurant Mamma Angela at the sea?)*
Le piacerebbe mangiare una pizza al ristorante Mamma Angela al mare?

Now it's your turn. Use the suggestions in the brackets.

- ▶ Le piacerebbe ...?   *(a ticket to Riva and a hotel on Lake Garda)*
- ▶ Le piacerebbe andare ...?   *(by plane to Rome with six nice friends)*
- ▶ Le piacerebbe essere ...?   *(in Florence from May until September)*
- ▶ Le piacerebbe vedere ...?   *(this photo of my red Ferrari)*

- ▶ Le piacerebbe comprare …? *(a shop or a restaurant in London)*
- ▶ Le piacerebbe riparare (repair) …? *(my car which I bought for 1,000 euros)*
- ▶ Le piacerebbe lavorare …? *(in a new shop in the centre of Milan)*
- ▶ Le piacerebbero …? *(the pizzas at the airport)*

Day 4

◄ CD2, TR 26

WHAT TO DO TODAY

✓ Read the five **New words**
✓ Read and work out the **Story** and the **New sentences**
✓ Listen to and speak along with the **CD**
✓ Learn today's five **New words** and the **New sentences** by heart
✓ **Let's speak Italian!** One easy speaking exercise
✓ Check your progress with the **CD**

The story
(In autostrada)

Carlo   Mi dispiace, credo che abbiamo un problema. Ah, mamma mia! Non ho benzina!

Gina   C'è un'uscita dell'autostrada laggiù e una fermata dell'autobus. E qui – c'è l'autobus!

Paul   Due per l'aeroporto, per favore.

Mario   *(The driver)* Andata e ritorno?

Paul   No, no, solo andata.

Today's new words

l'autostrada	*the motorway*
la benzina	*the petrol*
l'uscita	*the exit*
la fermata	*the stop*
andata e ritorno	*return ticket*

Today's new sentences

Un biglietto di andata e ritorno? Otto euro. La benzina? Dodici euro. La fermata dell'autobus? Qui vicino all'uscita dell'autostrada. Altro?

LET'S SPEAK ITALIAN!

Have another look at the last two pieces of dialogue, Days 3 and 4. Then answer these questions in whole sentences, still speaking OUT LOUD!

Day 3

▸ Perché non vuole andare in Inghilterra Claire?
▸ Quando deve lavorare?
▸ Com'è il tempo a Birmingham in aprile?
▸ Come vanno all'aeroporto?

Day 4

▸ Perché ha un problema in autostrada Carlo?
▸ Paul non compra quattro biglietti per l'aeroporto. Perché no?
▸ Paul compra i biglietti di andata e ritorno?
▸ Perché non compra biglietti di andata e ritorno?
▸ Dov'è la fermata dell'autobus?
▸ Che cosa devono fare con la macchina Carlo e Gina?

Day 5

WHAT TO DO TODAY

✓ Read the five **New words**
✓ Read and work out the **Story** and the **New sentences**
✓ Listen to and speak along with the **CD**
✓ Learn today's five **New words** and the **New sentences** by heart
✓ **Let's speak Italian!** Two easy speaking exercises
✓ Check your progress with the **CD**

The story
(In aereo)

Paul Abbiamo mangiato. Che cosa possiamo fare adesso?
C'è un giornale?

Claire Non abbiamo visto le foto!

Paul Ecco qui! Mi piace la foto della casa che era troppo cara,
la foto del mare senza tutta la gente e la foto di Tom, ieri,
dopo una bottiglia di vino.

Claire *Una* bottiglia? ... Ieri? Erano un po' di più ... come due
o tre ...

Today's new words

un giornale	*a newspaper*
senza	*without*
ieri	*yesterday*
dopo	*after, afterwards*
un po'	*a little*

Today's new sentences

Ieri era fantastico! Com'era? Che cosa ha fatto? Ho comprato un
giornale. E dopo, ha lavorato un po'? No. Dopo non ho fatto niente.

LET'S SPEAK ITALIAN!

1 Let's talk about today's dialogue. Answer in Italian, in full
sentences.

▶ Che cosa cerca in aereo Paul?
▶ Hanno visto le foto?
▶ C'è una foto del mare con molta gente?
▶ Chi è Tom?
▶ Quando hanno fatto la foto di Tom?
▶ Dopo quante bottiglie di vino hanno fatto la foto?

2 When you know your **New sentences** by heart give me these
variations:

▶ Yesterday the weather was bad.
▶ I like a little sun.
▶ I like to go to the seaside – with a newspaper.
▶ I like a little bar without many people.
▶ And then I like a large glass of red wine.

Day 6

◆) CD2, TR 28

WHAT TO DO TODAY

✓ Read the five **New words**
✓ Read and work out the **Story** and the **New sentences**
✓ Listen to and speak along with the **CD**
✓ Learn today's five **New words** and the **New sentences** by heart
✓ **Let's speak Italian!** Two easy speaking exercises
✓ Check your progress with the **CD**

The story

Paul   Che cosa c'è?

Claire   Le foto di Firenze sono troppo piccole. E perché tre foto del benzinaio? E chi è la signora in bikini?

Paul   Mi dispiace. Sì, sono foto brutte. Ma – ho un'idea fantastica! L'anno prossimo andiamo in Francia! Ho un amico all'Air France. Ha una casa a …

Claire   Andiamo!

Today's new words

il benzinaio, da un benzinaio	*the petrol station, to/at a petrol station*
un'idea	*an idea*
l'anno	*the year*
prossimo	*next*
Francia, la Francia	*France*

Today's new sentences

In Francia lavoro da un benzinaio – con mia moglie. Adesso ho una buona idea. L'anno prossimo lavoriamo da un benzinaio in Italia e – parliamo italiano!

LET'S SPEAK ITALIAN!

1 Take out this week's five **Flash sentences** and test yourself –
  speaking OUT LOUD until you are word perfect.

2 Have another look at today's **Story**. Decide if these statements
  are right or wrong. Then respond to them in Italian, in whole
  sentences starting with **sì** or **no**.

▶ Paul and Claire have eaten on the plane.
▶ Claire wants to see the photos.
▶ They only have a few photos.
▶ The photos of Florence are too small.
▶ Did Paul take two photos of the petrol station?
▶ Is there a photo of a woman in a bikini?
▶ Does Paul want to go to Ibiza next?
▶ Do Paul and Claire speak more Italian now?

Day 7

◆) CD2, TR 29

It's the last day of your course! Today you'll receive your
Certificate. Today you could catch a plane to Venice and follow
in the footsteps of Paul and Claire, speaking Italian – all the time!
But first there's some work to be finished.

WHAT TO DO TODAY

✓ Before you start on the **Story** open the **Traveller's companion**.
The **Mini-dictionary** shows all 210 words which you have
learned during the past seven weeks. Just in case you get stuck ...

✓ Enjoy reading the final complete **Story**. It's the longest one
ever. There are over 250 words, and you know them all

✓ Work through the final exercises which follow

✓ Add up your points for this week and then calculate your
overall course result

✓ Fill in your **Certificate**. It will spell out how well you have
done

Congratulations!

Here's this week's whole story

Paul   Non lo credo! È già sabato. Solo più un giorno di vacanza.
Che cosa facciamo oggi?

Claire   Voglio comprare qualcosa di bello per il mio direttore –
all'Upim.

Paul   Voglio fare delle foto – non abbiamo una foto di noi due.
Chi può aiutare? C'è qualcuno che ...?

Claire   *(Turning to a stranger)* Ah, scusi, può aiutarmi, per favore,
a fare una foto? Sì, con mio marito, qui, a tavola.

(The next day)

Claire   È domenica. Arrivederci Italia! Non mi piace andare in
Inghilterra. C'è brutto tempo là e lunedì devo lavorare.

Gina   Ma Birmingham è interessante, no?

(Contd)

Carlo	Ecco la mia macchina. Andiamo all'aeroporto. Non abbiamo molto tempo.
(In autostrada)	
Carlo	Mi dispiace, credo che abbiamo un problema. Ah, mamma mia! Non ho benzina!
Gina	C'è un'uscita dell'autostrada laggiù e una fermata dell'autobus. E qui – c'è l'autobus!
Paul	Due per l'aeroporto, per favore.
Mario	*(The driver)* Andata e ritorno?
Paul	No, no, solo andata.
(In aereo)	
Paul	Abbiamo mangiato. Che cosa possiamo fare adesso? C'è un giornale?
Claire	Non abbiamo visto le foto!
Paul	Ecco qui! Mi piace la foto della casa che era troppo cara, la foto del mare senza tutta la gente e la foto di Tom, ieri, dopo una bottiglia di vino.
Claire	*Una* bottiglia? … Ieri? Erano un po' di più … come due o tre …
Paul	Che cosa c'è?
Claire	Le foto di Firenze sono troppo piccole. E perché tre foto del benzinaio? E chi è la signora in bikini?
Paul	Mi dispiace. Sì, sono foto brutte. Ma – ho un'idea fantastica! L'anno prossimo andiamo in Francia! Ho un amico all'Air France. Ha una casa a …
Claire	Andiamo!

And now for the final test on your progress!

LAST WORD CHECK

Take out the 60 **Flash cards** from Weeks 3 and 4. Do you still remember the words which you learned some time ago? Spread them out with the English facing you. Close your eyes and pick 20 cards at random. Now give the Italian for each one. Score a maximum of 20 points.

Do the next four exercises with your tutor on the **CD** and with a
pen in your hand to write down your score.

TELL ME, TELL ME ...

Remember what happened? You may look at the **Story** if you
don't. Answer in Italian – and of course speak OUT LOUD! Give
yourself three points for each easy answer, two points for a bit
of a struggle and one point for a good attempt.

- ▶ Quando devono andare in Inghilterra Paul e Claire?
- ▶ Che cosa vuole fare Claire?
- ▶ Che cosa vuole fare Paul?
- ▶ Com'è il tempo in Inghilterra?
- ▶ C'è qualcuno che può aiutare a fare qualcosa. Che cosa?
- ▶ Chi è nella foto a tavola?
- ▶ Come vanno all'aeroporto i quattro amici?
- ▶ Che problema hanno nell'autostrada?
- ▶ Dove vogliono andare l'anno prossimo Paul e Claire?
- ▶ Perché?

QUICK SENTENCES

Here are five short, useful sentences from this week's text. Say
them quickly in Italian. Score two points for a fast sentence and
one for normal speed.

- ▶ Who is it?
- ▶ What are we going to do?
- ▶ Can you help me, please?
- ▶ I believe we have a problem.
- ▶ A return ticket, please.

VERBS, VERBS!

Say these verbs and verb phrases in Italian.

> to arrive, I cannot work, we worked, he was (has been),
> they bought, it is finished, I don't know, can you help me?,
> can you speak more slowly, please?, she went, I have
> said, you saw, I believe that ..., I cannot drink, I want to
> call, we cannot, would you like to have, how much does it
> cost?, I am looking for ..., I don't have it

Score one point for each correct verb or phrase.

THE STORY OF PAUL AND CLAIRE

On Day 7 of each of the seven weeks of this **Starter kit** the **Story**
for the week is given in full.

Tell me in Italian, in one or two sentences, what each Day 7 **Story**
is about.

1 Andiamo in Italia
2 Dov'è Gina?
3 Voglio una casa ... a Venezia!
4 Andiamo a Firenze
5 Alla pizzeria
6 Devo andare dal medico
7 Arrivederci Italia ... ma abbiamo le foto!

Score between ten and 20 points depending on how well you think
you spoke.

Now for your final results ...

YOUR FINAL RESULT

- ✓ Last word check   /20
- ✓ Remember what happened?   /30
- ✓ Quick sentences   /10
- ✓ Verbs, verbs!   /20
- ✓ The story of Paul and Claire   /20

Total score   **/100%   Date _____**

Enter your final result on the **Progress chart**. Then write your name on your **Certificate**.

You can now speak Starter kit Italian!

Credits

Front cover: © Oxford Designer and Illustrators Ltd

Back cover and pack: © Jakub Semeniuk/iStockphoto.com,
© Royalty-Free/Corbis, © agencyby/iStockphoto.com, © Andy
Cook/iStockphoto.com, © Christopher Ewing/iStockphoto.com,
© zebicho – Fotolia.com, © Geoffrey Holman/iStockphoto.com,
© Photodisc/Getty Images, © James C. Pruitt/iStockphoto.com,
© Mohamed Saber – Fotolia.com

Pack: © Stockbyte/Getty Images

*This is to certify
that*

....

*has successfully completed
the seven-week*

*Italian
starter kit*

course with _____ *results*

Elizabeth Smith

Tutor

Date